The Effects of the Minimum Wage on Employment

The Effects of the Minimum Wage on Employment

Edited by Marvin H. Kosters

The AEI Press

Publisher for the American Enterprise Institute
WASHINGTON, D.C.

1996

Available in the United States from the AEI Press, c/o Publisher Resources Inc., 1224 Heil Quaker Blvd., P.O. Box 7001, La Vergne, TN 37086-7001. Distributed outside the United States by arrangement with Eurospan, 3 Henrietta Street, London WC2E 8LU England.

Library of Congress Cataloging-in-Publication Data

The effects of the minimum wage on employment / edited by
  Marvin H. Kosters.
      p.   cm.
    Includes bibliographical references and index.
    ISBN 0-8447-7047-7 (paper).—ISBN 0-8447-7064-7 (cloth)
    1. Minimum wage—United States.   2. Labor market—
  United States.   3. Employment (Economic theory)
  I. Kosters, Marvin H.
  HD4918.E37   1996
  331.12′0973—dc20   96-34644
                                                                        CIP

1   3   5   7   9   10   8   6   4   2

The AEI Press
Publisher for the American Enterprise Institute
1150 17th Street, N.W., Washington, D.C. 20036

Printed in the United States of America

Contents

Preface

The Clinton administration's proposal in early 1995 to increase the minimum wage renewed interest in the question of how job creation would be affected. The president's proposal came at a time when academic interest in the effects of the minimum wage on employment was rekindled by David Card and Alan B. Krueger, whose book, *Myth and Measurement: The New Economics of the Minimum Wage* (1995), challenged the consensus among labor market economists that increasing the minimum wage would reduce employment of teenagers and other low-wage workers.

Since at least the beginning of the 1980s, most economists regarded the issue of whether the minimum wage has adverse effects on employment as settled, although there were differences about the magnitude of the negative effects. Several studies emerged in the early 1990s that raised questions about the strength and significance of employment effects. In their book, Card and Krueger drew on their own research and related work by others to argue that recent, modest increases in the minimum wage have had no significant adverse effects on employment.

Labor market specialists who have done research on the effects of the minimum wage have different views about what the evidence shows, and they also disagree about how apparent differences in results should be interpreted. Proponents of the new view of minimum-wage effects have been sharply critical of much of the research underlying the earlier consensus. They argue that their research evidence showing no negative effects on employment calls for not just a modest revision of the estimated size of minimum wage effects, but a reassessment of the labor market theories underlying the conventional view. Those who are skeptical of the new view have found the arguments and evidence presented by its proponents unpersuasive, and they point to other research analyzing recent experience that supports the conventional view of minimum-wage effects. Instead of moving professional opinion toward a new consensus, the new minimum-wage research seems to have contributed to increased polarization of views among the leading experts.

To develop a clearer understanding of the reasons for disagreement among experts about what research on minimum-wage effects shows, the American Enterprise Institute held a seminar in Washington on June 1, 1995, to examine the evidence. Leading scholars presented their analysis, critiqued different research approaches, and discussed how disparate results should be interpreted. Charles Brown, David Card, Alan B. Krueger, Kevin M. Murphy, David Neumark, and Finis R. Welch were asked to make presentations. Participants in the seminar included mainly labor market specialists, many of whom had done research on minimum-wage issues. This publication, like the seminar on which it is based, is intended to make perspectives on issues discussed in the seminar available to a broader audience.

This book includes a brief introductory overview, a summary of evidence developed by David Card and Alan Krueger, a chapter by Donald Deere, Kevin M. Murphy, and Finis Welch presenting their analysis, a chapter written by David Neumark and William Wascher, a chapter written by Charles Brown, and a final chapter with my conclusions. David Card and Alan Krueger decided not to participate in this publication. The summary of their evidence that I have written, included here as chapter 2, draws almost entirely on their book and quotes liberally from it. I regret that they decided not to write up their presentations and to discuss their evidence in the context of other views that were presented, but I am very grateful to them for participating in the seminar.

The reasons that Card and Krueger give for their decision not to participate in the AEI minimum-wage volume follow.

> First, we believe that our research on the minimum wage and our conclusions from this research are carefully laid out in our own book. Second, we feel that the volume may inadvertently give an unfair slant to our work. Our research tries to address basic research concerns about the functioning of the labor market: our research makes no policy recommendation about raising (or eliminating) the minimum wage. Other papers in the volume have a more normative approach. We also believe that the form and composition of the volume will give credence to the claim that we are on the "fringe" of economics—a claim that we strongly dispute but that is conveyed by the tone and content of the other papers. Finally, we are extremely unhappy about the Neumark and Wascher contribution. They have refused to make available the data used in their paper, even though they used our data, and even though their paper makes very strong claims about the relative quality of their data. Although we could conceive of a valuable exchange in which we reevaluate our analysis in light of their data, that is not possible.[1]

In my introductory overview, I have highlighted what I regard as the main ideas and arguments presented at the seminar. In the chapter summarizing Card and Krueger's arguments and evidence, I have adhered as closely as pos-

---

1. Letter dated October 3, 1995, signed by David Card and Alan Krueger.

sible to the presentation in their book and sent the material I wrote to them and invited their review and comments. As is apparent when my overview is compared with my summary of the views presented in their book, Card and Krueger both emphasized in their presentation at the seminar the similarity of their empirical results to an earlier consensus view. Finally, in the concluding chapter I summarize my views about the evidence on employment effects of the minimum wage. I do not claim to be a neutral observer, but I hope I have summarized fairly the evidence that Card and Krueger present in their book and the discussion at the AEI seminar.

Contributors

MARVIN H. KOSTERS is a resident scholar and the director of economic policy studies at the American Enterprise Institute. He served as a senior economist to the President's Council of Economic Advisers and at the White House office of the assistant to the president for economic affairs. Mr. Kosters is the coeditor of *Trade and Wages: Leveling Wages Down?* (AEI Press, 1994) and is the editor of *Personal Saving, Consumption, and Tax Policy* (AEI Press, 1992) and *Workers and Their Wages* (AEI Press, 1991). Mr. Kosters has contributed to *American Economic Review* and *The Public Interest.*

CHARLES C. BROWN is a professor of economics at the University of Michigan, Ann Arbor. He is also a research associate at the National Bureau of Economic Research, and he is a member of the editorial boards of the *American Economic Review* and the *Journal of Economic Literature.* Mr. Brown has published several articles in professional journals on labor market issues and is a coauthor of *Employers Large and Small.*

DONALD R. DEERE is associate professor of economics at Texas A&M University, and associate director for academic programs at its George Bush School of Government and Public Service. His research on labor market issues has been published in several professional journals.

KEVIN M. MURPHY is the George Pratt Shultz Professor of Business Economics and Industrial Relations at the University of Chicago, where he has been a faculty member since 1982. He is also a faculty research associate at the National Bureau of Economic Research. Mr. Murphy has written numerous articles on labor and wage issues.

DAVID NEUMARK joined the faculty of Michigan State University as a professor in the Department of Economics in 1994. His fields of study include labor economics and econometrics. He was an economic consultant for Abt Associates, Inc., and an economist in the division of research and statistics for the board of governors of the Federal Reserve System. Mr. Neumark has written extensively on labor market issues.

WILLIAM WASCHER is a senior economist with the Board of Governors of the Federal Reserve System, where he specializes in labor economics and macroeconomic forecasting. He served as a senior economist with the President's Council of Economic Advisers from 1989 to 1990. He is the author or coauthor of a number of articles on wage and price determination, productivity, and other labor market issues.

FINIS R. WELCH is the Abell Professor of Liberal Arts and Distinguished Professor of Economics at Texas A&M University. Mr. Welch was a research fellow at the National Bureau of Economic Research and has conducted a significant amount of research on the employment effects of minimum wages. Mr. Welch has been published in numerous professional journals and has testified before congressional committees and governmental agencies.

1
Introduction and Overview

Marvin H. Kosters

The most obvious direct effect of increasing the minimum wage is to raise the incomes of low-wage workers with jobs, and it is probably not surprising that raising the minimum wage usually meets with an overwhelmingly favorable response in opinion polls. Popular opinion is more mixed on how high the minimum wage should be, however. The question of how much to raise the minimum wage apparently gives rise to concerns about the effects on costs to employers, and consequently to concerns about inflation and about jobs.

The question of whether the minimum wage discourages employment and, if so, then by how much is the issue that has dominated public discussion of minimum-wage policy. It is usually taken for granted that those whose wages are increased by a minimum-wage hike would be better off, assuming they keep their jobs, even though other changes required by their employers might offset part of the benefit of higher money earnings. Few workers might actually lose their jobs; in most instances simply not replacing all those who leave can soon achieve a similar outcome. Those who may be harmed by increased difficulty in getting a job cannot easily trace their problem to a higher minimum wage. Under these circumstances, the strategy taken by many elected officials has been to embrace the minimum wage in principle, to take advantage of the political rewards of raising it periodically, but to

1

avoid raising it so much that the consequences for employment are too apparent or severe.

The federal Minimum Wage Study Commission created in 1977 was directed to study a number of minimum-wage policy issues. When the commission submitted its report in 1981, the issue that received the most public attention was the employment effects of the minimum wage.[1] The research sponsored by the commission or stimulated by its work helped to establish the basis for a consensus among economists about the effects of the minimum wage on employment.

The conclusions of their research on the employment issue are summarized in a paper by Charles Brown, Curtis Gilroy, and Andrew Kohen, who served as senior economists on the staff of the commission.[2] In their summary the authors say: "Time-series studies typically find that a 10 percent increase in the minimum wage reduces teenage employment by 1 to 3 percent. . . . We believe that the lower half of the range is to be preferred."[3] This often quoted statement expressed a consensus among economists that was quite widely accepted among experts and commentators as a basis for informed discussion of minimum-wage effects. Some disagreement remained about how large the adverse effects on employment were, but lower employment was regarded as a price that had to be paid to obtain an increase in the minimum wage.

A series of studies emerged in the early 1990s, raising questions about the validity of the proposition that raising the minimum made it more difficult for some workers to get jobs and led to reduced employment. The most influential of these studies was carried out by David Card and Alan Krueger. It compared changes in employment in

---

1. *Report of the Minimum Wage Study Commission*, vol. 1, May 1981.

2. Charles Brown, Curtis Gilroy, and Andrew Kohen, "The Effect of the Minimum Wage on Employment and Unemployment," *Journal of Economic Literature*, June 1982, vol. 20, pp. 487–528.

3. Ibid., p. 524.

fast-food restaurants in New Jersey and Pennsylvania, to examine the effects of a minimum wage that was raised in New Jersey but not in Pennsylvania.[4] The conclusion of the study—that comparative employment performance was not harmed in New Jersey—received a great deal of popular attention, partly perhaps because the comparisons it made seemed straightforward and persuasive.

These studies claiming that modest increases in the minimum wage appeared to have no significant negative effects on employment attracted considerably more public attention when the Clinton administration appealed to evidence from this new body of research to argue that its proposed minimum-wage increase would not hurt job prospects of less-skilled workers. Much of the increased attention to the new minimum-wage research was focused on Professors Card and Krueger, whose new book putting forth their view of the evidence was published soon after the proposed increase in the minimum wage was announced. The book presented the results of their research in considerable detail and reexamined some of the earlier research that produced different conclusions. The authors left little doubt that they viewed the results of their analysis as being sharply at variance with the consensus view.

Both the Card and Krueger book and the findings reported by the Minimum Wage Study Commission represent important statements about research on the employment effects of the minimum wage. In contrast with the commission report, which reflected broad agreement among researchers about the evidence from empirical research at that time, however, the views and conclusions expressed by Card and Krueger in their book do not represent a consensus among minimum-wage specialists now.

---

4. This study was published in the *American Economic Review:* "Minimum Wages and Employment: A Case Study of the Fast-Food Industry in New Jersey and Pennsylvania," September 1994, vol. 84, pp. 772–93.

It is accordingly a controversial statement, and its conclusions are sharply contested by other analysts whose research shows adverse employment effects.

Highlights of the Seminar on Employment Effects of the Minimum Wage

In his presentation, Alan Krueger indicated that their conclusion that the minimum wage has little or no effect on employment does not differ as much from earlier research as has sometimes been suggested. He argued that the negative effects on employment of increases in the minimum wage were fairly small in earlier studies, and that their research suggests that those effects are even smaller.

Krueger concentrated primarily on the effects of an increase in the minimum wage on employment in a sample of fast-food restaurants. Their most widely publicized study compared employment changes in New Jersey, where the state legal minimum wage was increased in 1992, with Pennsylvania, where it was not. Analysis of the effects of this difference in policies was appealing as a case study because anticipatory employment adjustments might be expected to be small in view of uncertainty about whether the new minimum wage in New Jersey would actually go into effect as scheduled on April 1. Furthermore, there was a high concentration of relatively low-wage teenage workers in fast-food restaurants, and turnover was high, so that employment levels could be adjusted relatively quickly.

Card and Krueger's results, presented in detail in their book, did not show a decline in fast-food employment in New Jersey relative to Pennsylvania. The average fast-food restaurant in Pennsylvania had more employees than in New Jersey in early 1992, but later in the year—after the minimum wage had been increased in New Jersey—restaurants in both states employed about the same

4

number of workers. Several ways of analyzing the data showed small positive employment differences in New Jersey, but since the estimates are not statistically significant, neither small negative employment effects nor small positive employment effects can be rejected.

Krueger responded to criticisms that have been raised about the validity of the data they collected by explaining the methods they used and discussing evidence on the reliability of their data in relation to data from other sources. He pointed out that reporting errors need not necessarily lead to bias in estimates of employment effects. Moreover, data from some other sources are consistent with the differences in employment trends they found between Pennsylvania and New Jersey.

David Card acknowledged that studies of employment in a narrow sector of the economy, such as fast-food restaurants, have limitations. He described their analyses of differences across states in the proportions of workers who would be affected by an increase in the federal minimum wage. Wage levels and wage distributions for teenagers in different states are very different, and imposing a uniform standard when the federal minimum was increased in 1990 and 1991 would be expected to have quite different effects. Moreover, some states, such as California, had already raised their minimum wage to levels above the prevailing federal rate.

Their analysis was carried out by estimating the fraction of teenagers who were earning a wage between the old federal minimum and the new one. This fraction varies substantially among states, and their analysis shows that imposition of a national minimum pushes up wages more in states where more teenagers were initially below the standard. Although demand for teenage workers might be expected to decrease in response to higher wages, employment rates of teenagers did not appear to be reduced more in states where their average wages were pushed up most. Efforts to take into account broader employment

5

trends or regional differences did not change the picture much, nor did extending the time period for adjustment to minimum-wage increases.

He also discussed other analyses across states in which they examined total employment in the retail trade and restaurant industries, with results that were similar to those for teenagers. Estimates of the size and statistical significance of minimum wage effects on employment in these industry sectors were quite sensitive to other variables included in the analysis, but the estimated effects were small and positive. The imprecision of many of the estimates means that the possibility of small negative effects cannot be entirely ruled out, according to Card, but their studies lead them to conclude that the employment effects of the minimum wage were relatively small at the end of the 1980s.

Finis Welch began by noting that economic theory has increasingly been brought to bear on analysis of labor markets, and one of the most robust predictions of economic theory is the law of demand. Applied to the minimum-wage issue, the prediction is straightforward; higher minimum wages imply less employment. If this were a shortcut to improving incomes, why not just increase the minimum wage and save on investments in education, training, technology, and infrastructure?

The attention given to the Card and Krueger results and Welch's skepticism about their validity led him, with Donald Deere and Kevin Murphy, to examine the employment effects of the 1990 and 1991 federal minimum-wage increases. The results of their analysis are broadly consistent with the earlier consensus of significant negative effects on employment. Welch raised the following question: if the law of demand is as robust as he and many other economists contend, why do some studies by Card, Krueger, and others get either anomalous or contradictory results?

One reason employment effects can be difficult to

isolate is that the effect on labor costs of an increase in the minimum wage is often small in relation to other changes going on at the same time and in relation to sampling error. Welch illustrated this problem by calculating that the average cost to employ teenagers increased by about 1.5 percent when the minimum wage was increased in April 1990 from $3.35 to $3.80 (a 13.4 percent increase), and the total increase from $3.35 to $4.25 (in two steps in 1990 and 1991) raised average teenage employment cost by only 3 to 4 percent. Since changes in teenage wages in a single month are typically on the order of 2 percent or more, however, the employment effects of a minimum-wage change may not be easy to see in a simple comparison for a sample from one sector of the economy.

Kevin M. Murphy noted that minimum-wage research has historically focused on teenagers because it would be extremely difficult to isolate the much smaller effect of a rise in the minimum wage on the price of labor for the economy as a whole. Even for teenagers, he argued, we have to look for the effects of relatively small changes in a world with a lot of noise, some of it systematic. Teenage employment rates, for example, were about the same in New Jersey and Pennsylvania in 1988, but the rate in New Jersey declined by more than 9 percentage points compared with Pennsylvania by 1991. This difference is so large compared with a difference of 1.6 percentage points (in the opposite direction) in 1992 that something else was obviously going on that was systematically different between these two states.

Comparisons across states of employment rates for twenty-five to fifty-year-old men with more than twelve years of schooling—a group quite insulated from minimum-wage effects—show that employment was growing much more rapidly in low-wage states, basically Sunbelt states in the South and Southwest, than in the rest of the country. Systematic differences among states have to be taken into account in order to trace differences in employment experience to causes such as an increase in the minimum wage. This problem is very similar to the need to take into account the influence of the business cycle and other factors in time-series studies, studies that examine the effects on employment of periodic increases in the dollar value of the minimum wage that interrupted gradual erosion of real minimum-wage levels because of inflation.

Murphy also noted that raising the minimum wage does not make anybody better off without someone else paying for it. Many of those who have to pay the higher prices that result from a minimum-wage increase have incomes much like those who get a higher wage. Since many of the poor are not working, part of the benefit to low-wage workers of a higher minimum wage comes at the expense of nonworking poor consumers. Moreover, even if net disemployment effects are small, people with the hardest time getting a job will lose out in comparison with those whose earning capabilities are a little higher.

Some of the favorable public discussion of Card and Krueger's research suggests that what they did represents a methodological breakthrough based on natural experiments. But the problems of bias and omitted variables that plague the time-series studies are also present in the new studies. Murphy concluded that the evidence from these new studies does not change his view about the negative employment effects of raising the minimum wage.

David Neumark, with his coauthor William Wascher, analyzed the effects of minimum-wage changes across states. They found significant negative effects on employment. Their results for teenagers are sensitive to the ways school enrollment is measured and school enrollment decisions are taken into account. This led them to examine the effects of the minimum wage on both work and school choices.

Neumark explained that the small net employment effects of the minimum wage reflect partially offsetting shifts in school and employment status. Their results indicate that raising the minimum wage shifts employer demand from the least-skilled teenagers to those with slightly better skills. As a result, teenagers with somewhat better skills increase their working hours by going from being in school and employed to being out of school and employed. Some of the least-skilled teenagers, however, are priced out of the labor market, and their status changes from out-of-school and employed to neither in school nor employed.

By using methods that estimate the likelihood that a worker's wages are actually affected by an increase in the minimum wage, Neumark and Wascher's analysis helps to reconcile disparate results that have been reported. Their estimates show that in a high-wage state like California, where the probability of being affected by minimum wages is quite low, the estimated effects on employment should also be expected to be small.

Neumark and Wascher also analyzed data from payroll records for a sample of fast-food restaurants in New Jersey and Pennsylvania. Using these data they estimated that a 10 percent increase in the minimum wage reduced employment by about 2 percent, a result consistent with their other studies. Neumark and Wascher conclude that the conventional economic model of low-wage labor markets and its prediction for the employment effects of minimum wages have not been contradicted by the new revisionist evidence.

Charles Brown began by reviewing the "old" economics of the minimum wage. He pointed out that time-series estimates were clustered in a fairly narrow range, and they were not sensitive to whether hours of work or employment were examined, or to different sets of control variables. He acknowledged that analyses that extend through the 1980s produced smaller estimated effects. Other puzzles left by that research include why the evidence did not consistently show black employment more strongly affected than white, and why extension of coverage to industries that were not previously subject to the minimum wage did not show more noticeable effects. In most of the earlier research the level and coverage of the minimum wage were combined in a fairly crude way, and estimated employment effects apparently mainly reflected the influence of changes in the minimum wage level.

Examination of a particular sector of the economy, or comparison between sectors affected differently by the minimum wage, is not a new analytic approach, according to Brown. In some of the studies examined by the staff of the Minimum Wage Study Commission, employment fell in sectors most affected by the minimum wage, but in others the results were mixed. Although these earlier studies were conceptually similar, those carried out by Card and Krueger used much more sophisticated analytical tools.

Estimates of minimum-wage effects are apparently sensitive to the length of time allowed for adjustment to take place. Efforts to pick up more of the cumulative employment effects, however, are also likely to be more strongly affected by statistical noise and preexisting trends.

Estimates of the negative effects on employment of an increase in the minimum wage are fairly small. This should not be surprising because the effect on average wages of an increase in the minimum wage, even for groups most affected such as teenagers, has also usually been quite small. In addition, the net change in employment reflects offsetting changes for gainers and losers. Brown concludes in evaluating the empirical evidence that the new minimum wage studies are subject to many of the same limitations and methodological problems as the older studies.

2

A Summary of the New Economics of the Minimum Wage

Marvin H. Kosters

In their book *Myth and Measurement: The New Economics of the Minimum Wage,* David Card and Alan B. Krueger present what is described on the book jacket as "a powerful new challenge to the conventional view that higher minimum wages reduce jobs for low-wage workers."[1] The purpose of this chapter is to describe and summarize the evidence they develop on the employment effects of the minimum wage: the main features of the labor market experiences they examine, the essentials of the arguments they make, and central results of the analyses they carry out. Readers who are interested in the authors' own exposition are encouraged to consult their book, a careful reading of which is essential to the full appreciation of the scope and detail of their analysis.

The new analysis of labor market experience presented by Card and Krueger involves comparisons of two kinds: among fast-food restaurants and among states. Each kind of comparison consists of one component that can be regarded as analysis of the main experiment and the other as a secondary or subsidiary experiment. The main experiment in their examination of the effects of the minimum wage on employment in fast-food restaurants is

---

1. David Card and Alan B. Krueger (1995).

11

a comparison of experience for restaurants in Pennsylvania and New Jersey when the state minimum wage was increased in New Jersey in 1992. The subsidiary experiment is an analysis of differences in the effects on fast-food restaurants in Texas of the increase in the federal minimum wage in 1991. The main experiment in their comparisons among states is an analysis of differences among states in the effects of increases in the federal minimum wage in 1990 and 1991, and a subsidiary analysis looks at the effects of an increase in the state minimum wage in California in 1988. In addition to developing and presenting these analyses, they critique the methodology and results of other major studies of the employment effects of the minimum wage and the conventional models of employment effects.

Evidence from the Fast-Food Industry

I begin by describing Card and Krueger's comparison of fast-food employment in New Jersey and Pennsylvania, because this study has received the most public attention and because, after an introduction and overview chapter, they begin the substantive part of their book by discussing this study.[2] On April 1, 1992, the state minimum wage in New Jersey was increased from $4.25 (the level of the federal minimum wage since April 1991) to $5.05, while the applicable legal minimum in Pennsylvania remained at $4.25. They argue that this increase in the minimum wage in New Jersey is particularly appealing as a natural experiment, because whether it would be allowed to take effect as scheduled under legislation enacted earlier remained uncertain until its effective date.

To examine how employment might be affected by the New Jersey minimum-wage increase, Card and Krueger collected data on employment from a sample of

2. Ibid., chapter 2.

about 400 fast-food restaurants in New Jersey and Pennsylvania. The data they collected were used to construct measures of full-time equivalent employment (FTE), hourly wages, prices, and so forth. The fast-food outlets were contacted by telephone during late February and early March 1992, shortly before the April 1 minimum-wage increase in New Jersey, and again in November and December 1992. Reasons they give for looking at the fast-food industry include: the industry employs many low-wage workers; industry compliance with the law is expected to be high; jobs and services are fairly homogeneous; a sample frame is fairly easy to design; earlier experience with Texas suggested high response rates; and high turnover of jobs facilitates rapid employment adjustment.

If we abstract from some well-known qualifications, the conventional analysis of how employment would be affected by an increase in the minimum wage is quite straightforward. Other things being equal, we would expect employment to fall in New Jersey in response to the increase in the legal minimum wage and to remain unchanged in Pennsylvania. Some qualifications might be important, of course, such as the possibility that other conditions affecting employment might have changed. Changes that have similar effects on employment in both states, however, would presumably not affect the difference in employment changes between the two states. It is this comparison of differences in changes that Card and Krueger examine, using what is called a "difference-in-differences" method.

The data they collected on fast-food restaurant employment suggest that everything else was apparently not equal. Instead of remaining the same, fast-food employment fell in Pennsylvania. More surprisingly, however, employment in fast-food restaurants actually increased in New Jersey instead of declining by more than in Pennsylvania. These results, expressed in terms of what happened to average employment per restaurant, are shown in fig-

FIGURE 2–1

Average Employment per Restaurant, before and after the Increase of the Minimum Wage

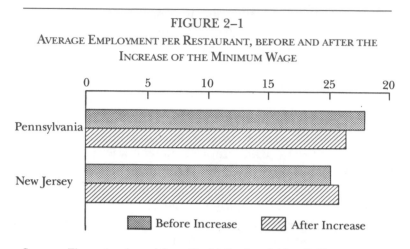

SOURCE: Figure is adapted from David Card and Alan B. Krueger, *Myth and Measurement: The New Economics of the Minimum Wage* (Princeton: Princeton University Press, 1995), p. 35.

ure 2–1.[3] The difference in changes in employment between the two states is not only in the opposite direction from what would be expected, but change takes place mainly in Pennsylvania. As John Kennan writes in his review, this result "is like having a drug trial in which the drug has no effect but the placebo makes people sick."[4]

Although this simple comparison describes the essence of what Card and Krueger found in their comparison of fast-food employment, other possible differences between the two states in the restaurants or in other conditions could have influenced relative employment. When they take a variety of other factors into account, the story remains pretty much the same. To illustrate some of their detailed analyses of the data they collected, the regression results reported in table 2–1 indicate the sensitivity of their results to differences in specification and to additional variables.[5]

3. Ibid., figure 2–3, panel A, p. 35.
4. John Kennan (1995), p. 1,958.
5. Card and Krueger, 1995, table 2.3, p. 38.

The results reported in the table are sufficiently well documented to be almost self-explanatory, but I will describe them briefly. A set of results for changes in employment measured in terms of numbers of workers that is reported in the first five columns is matched by a set based on proportional changes in employment in the second five columns. In the final two columns, the change in the starting wage is used as the dependent variable instead of employment changes. Differences between columns 1 through 5 (and columns 6 through 10) are of two kinds: the way the effects of the minimum wage are measured, and whether or not sets of variables for restaurant chains and locations of the outlets are included.

The estimated effects of the increase in the minimum wage in New Jersey are shown in the first two rows. The first measures the estimated effect of being located in New Jersey, while the second measures the estimated effect of the proportionate gap between the wage level required by the increase in the minimum wage in New Jersey and the previous starting wage. The estimated effects on employment are uniformly positive for all ten equations. For the first five equations, some of the coefficients appear statistically significant and others approach conventional levels of significance, although none of the coefficients in the second set of equations based on proportional employment changes are statistically significant. The size of the coefficients in the two sets of equations is of about the same order of magnitude after adjustment for the difference in magnitude of the dependent variables.

In addition to the examination of the effects of other factors reported in the table above, Card and Krueger look at estimated minimum wage effects for various subsets of their sample based on special circumstances surrounding the outlet or the interviews and based on the general location of the restaurants. They also look at possible differences in operating characteristics of restaurants (hours open, numbers of cash registers in operation, and

TABLE 2–1

EVIDENCE FROM THE FAST-FOOD INDUSTRY

	Dependent Variable: Change in Employment[a]				
	(1)	(2)	(3)	(4)	(5)
New Jersey dummy	2.33 (1.19)	2.30 (1.20)	—	—	—
Initial wage gap[d]	—	—	15.65 (6.08)	14.92 (6.21)	11.98 (7.42)
Controls for chain and ownership[e]	No	Yes	No	Yes	Yes
Controls for region[f]	No	No	No	No	Yes
Standard error of regression	8.79	8.78	8.76	8.76	8.75
Probability value for controls[g]	—	0.34	—	0.44	0.40

NOTE: Standard errors are shown in parentheses. The sample consists of 357 restaurants with nonmissing data on employment and starting wages in waves 1 and 2. All models include an unrestricted constant (not reported).
a. The dependent variable is the change in full-time-equivalent (FTE) employment. The mean and standard deviation of the dependent variable are –0.237 and 8.825, respectively.
b. The dependent variable is the change in FTE employment, divided by average employment in wave 1 and wave 2. For closed restaurants, proportional change = –1.0. The mean and standard deviation of the dependent variable are –0.005 and 0.374, respectively.
c. The dependent variable is the change in the starting wage, divided by the starting wage in wave 1. The mean and standard deviation of the dependent variable are 0.087 and 0.090, respectively.

TABLE 2-1 (continued)

	Dependent Variable: Proportional Change in Employment[b]				Dependent Variable: Proportional Change in Starting Wage[c]	
(6)	(7)	(8)	(9)	(10)	(11)	(12)
0.05 (0.05)	0.05 (0.05)	—	—	—	0.11 (0.01)	—
—	—	0.39 (0.26)	0.34 (0.26)	0.29 (0.31)	—	1.04 (0.03)
No	Yes	No	Yes	Yes	Yes	Yes
No	No	No	No	Yes	No	No
0.373	0.372	0.373	0.372	0.372	0.078	0.043
—	0.14	—	0.17	0.27	—	—

d. Proportional increase in starting wage necessary to increase starting wage to the new minimum rate. For restaurants in Pennsylvania, the wage gap is zero.

e. Dummy variables for chain type (three) and whether the restaurant is company owned are included.

f. Dummy variables for two regions of New Jersey and two regions of eastern Pennsylvania are included.

g. Probability value of joint F-test for exclusion of all control variables.

SOURCE: David Card and Alan B. Krueger, *Myth and Measurement: The New Economics of the Minimum Wage* (Princeton: Princeton University Press, 1995), p. 38, where it was entitled "Estimated Reduced-Form Models for Changes in Employment and Starting Wages."

so forth), nonwage conditions of employment (such as free meals), and wage profiles (such as time before receiving a raise). They examine the effects on prices in New Jersey of the minimum-wage increase. And they compare changes in broader measures of employment in New Jersey and Pennsylvania with changes in New York and the average for the United States. Little or no effect of the minimum wage is evident in any of these supplementary analyses.

Card and Krueger also discuss the effects of the 1988 increase in the minimum wage in Texas on employment in a sample of fast-food restaurants there. To estimate the effect of the minimum wage on employment, they rely on differences among restaurants within Texas in the gap between the wages a restaurant had to pay after the minimum wage was increased and the wages it had paid previously. This methodology is conceptually similar to their analysis of employment changes in New Jersey and Pennsylvania in relation to differences in the wage gap within New Jersey. The estimated results for Texas are also fairly similar to those for New Jersey, although the positive estimated coefficients appear statistically more significant for the Texas data.

What do Card and Krueger conclude from their results? It is useful to quote from some of their summary discussion. With regard to the simplest New Jersey-Pennsylvania comparison, they say: "Despite the increase in wages, FTE employment *increased* in New Jersey relative to Pennsylvania."[6] In a summary section following a discussion of their analysis in more detail, they say: "Regardless of whether low-wage restaurants in New Jersey are compared with those in Pennsylvania or with restaurants in New Jersey that already were paying as much as the new minimum wage, we find that the rise in the minimum wage seems to have *increased* employment. . . . At a mini-

---

6. Ibid., p. 33, authors' emphasis.

mum, we believe that our estimates call into question the prediction that an increase in the minimum wage will lead to significant employment losses at affected firms."[7] With regard to the analysis for Texas they say: "As was the case for New Jersey, the increase in the minimum wage in Texas was associated with a relative expansion in employment at firms that were forced to raise pay in order to comply with the law."[8] In summary, their results seem to suggest that employment effects are likely to be small, but more likely to be positive than negative.

Evidence from Cross-State Comparisons

Differences among states in the level and distribution of wages lead to corresponding differences in the effect on wage costs of an increase in the minimum wage.[9] In a second broad approach, Card and Krueger analyze the effects on employment of differences among states in the size of increases in wage costs implied by the federal minimum wage increases that took effect in April 1990 and April 1991. Wage levels differ among states because labor markets and living costs are different, and because by the late 1980s several states had set minimum wages above the level of the federal minimum. The resulting differences among states in the impetus to labor costs of a boost in the federal minimum wage can be examined to see if they were accompanied by systematic differences in employment patterns.

Several measures of employment by state are examined, usually in terms of changes from 1989 through 1992. Differences among states in the effect of an increase in the federal minimum wage are estimated as the gap between wages reported in CPS survey data and new federal

7. Ibid., pp. 45–46, authors' emphasis.

8. Ibid., p. 59.

9. Ibid., chapters 3 and 4.

minimum scheduled to go into effect. Examination of differences in employment among groups of states based on the size of the minimum-wage gap shows no clear evidence of effects. Results for their regression analysis for teenagers are reported in table 2–2.[10] These results show that although the estimated effect of the federal minimum wage on wage costs was substantial (columns 1 and 2), differences among states in the fraction of teenagers affected by increases in the federal minimum wage appear to have had no significant effect on teenagers' employment rates. This conclusion for teenagers' employment rates is buttressed by regressions that take into account several additional factors, such as changes in wages of adult men, annual employment rates, lagged teenage employment rates, state voting patterns, and regional effects.

Card and Krueger carry out a cross-state analysis similar to that for teenagers for employment in the relatively low-wage retail trade and restaurant industries. The results they report for the effect on wage costs show a pattern similar to those for teenagers.[11] The estimated effects on employment of workers affected by the federal minimum wage increases are uniformly positive, although their size and statistical significance are greatly diminished by variables designed to take into account differences in state employment conditions.

In addition to their cross-state analysis of the effects of the 1990 and 1991 increases in the federal minimum wage, they report on a conceptually similar analysis of the effects of the large increase in the state minimum wage in California in July 1988. Instead of a comparison across all states, however, what happened in California was compared with the United States as a whole and with a control group sample that included workers in Arizona, Florida, Georgia, New Mexico, and Dallas-Fort Worth, Texas. This

---

10. Ibid., table 4–4, p. 128.
11. See ibid., table 4–9, pp. 144–45.

TABLE 2-2
EVIDENCE FROM CROSS-STATE COMPARISONS

	Models for Change in Mean Log Wage		Models for Change in Employment Rate	
	(1)	(2)	(3)	(4)
A. Changes, April–December 1989 to April–December 1990				
Fraction of affected	0.15	0.14	0.02	–0.01
teenagers[a]	(0.03)	(0.04)	(0.03)	(0.03)
Change in overall	—	0.46	—	1.24
employment rate[b]		(0.60)		(0.60)
R-squared	0.30	0.31	0.01	0.09
B. Changes, April–December 1989 to April–December 1991				
Fraction of affected	0.29	0.24	0.13	0.04
teenagers[a]	(0.04)	(0.04)	(0.04)	(0.04)
Change in overall	—	1.03	—	1.69
employment rate[b]		(0.41)		(0.44)
R-squared	0.57	0.62	0.15	0.35
C. Changes, January–December 1989 to January–December 1992				
Fraction of affected	0.28	0.22	0.13	0.01
teenagers[a]	(0.04)	(0.05)	(0.03)	(0.03)
Change in overall	—	1.05	—	1.94
employment rate[b]		(0.51)		(0.31)
R-squared	0.58	0.62	0.31	0.62

NOTE: Standard errors are shown in parentheses. The models in panels A and B are estimated on 51 state-level observations (including the District of Columbia), using data derived from monthly Current Population Survey (CPS) samples for 1989–1991. The models in panel C are estimated on 50 state-level observations (excluding the District of Columbia), using wage data derived from CPS files for 1989 and 1992 and teenage employment rates taken from U.S. Department of Labor, *Geographic Profiles of Unemployment and Employment*. All models are estimated by weighted least squares, using the number of teenagers in the state in the 1989 CPS file as a weight.
a. Fraction of teenagers earning $3.35–3.79 per hour in the state (panel A) or $3.35–4.94 per hour (panels B and C) in 1989. In panels A and B, the fraction affected is estimated using data for April–December only. In panel C, the fraction affected is estimated using data for all 12 months of 1989.
b. The change in the overall employment-population rate for the state, taken from *Geographic Profiles of Unemployment and Employment*.
SOURCE: Ibid., table 4–4, p. 128. Original subtitle is "Estimated Regression Models for Changes in State Averages of Teenage Wages and Teenage Employment-Population Rates."

analysis uses comparisons of changes between 1987 and 1989 for teenagers and other demographic groups for the state as a whole and for retail trade and restaurant industries. Most of the evidence they discuss from their analysis of the California experience suggests a small positive relationship between employment and increased wage costs resulting from the increase in the legal minimum wage.

The conclusions that Card and Krueger draw from their comparisons across states are very much in line with those from their fast-food restaurant studies. In their judgment, "there is no evidence that the increase in the minimum wage significantly lowered teenage employment rates in more highly affected states."[12] Analysis of other workers likely to be affected by the minimum wage leads them to the same conclusion.[13] Although they acknowledge "we cannot rule out the possibility that the increase in the minimum wage had a small, negative effect on teenagers," they note in their discussion of industry employment effects that "our estimates for the restaurant industry suggest that employment actually increased *more rapidly* in states in which the federal minimum-wage hike generated the largest pay increases."[14] With regard to the California study, they indicate that the evidence "shows that the increase in the state minimum wage had a significant impact on wages, but no large or significant effect on employment."[15]

Summary of Evidence on Employment Effects

In their book, Card and Krueger address several other issues in addition to the evidence on the effects on employment of the minimum wage. They discuss anomalies

---

12. Ibid., p. 149.
13. Ibid., p. 149.
14. Ibid., pp. 137, 149, authors' emphasis.
15. Ibid., p. 110.

associated with the low wage labor market that they view as casting doubt on the validity of the textbook model of the minimum wage.[16] They examine distributional implications of the minimum wage and find that the minimum wage helped to offset the trend toward rising wage inequality. They suggest that news about increasing the minimum wage has had very little effect on the market value of firms that employ minimum wage workers. And their review and update of evidence from time series studies of the effect of minimum wage changes on teenage employment leads them to conclude that "the evidence showing the minimum wage has no effect or a positive effect on employment is at least as compelling as the evidence showing it has an adverse effect."[17] Their interpretation of their own research evidence on the employment effects of the minimum wage is well summarized in two paragraphs that I quote in their entirety below.[18]

> Our main empirical findings can be summarized as follows. First, a study of employment in the fast-food industry after the recent 1992 increase in the New Jersey minimum wage shows that employment was *not* affected by the law. Our results are derived from a specially designed survey of more than 400 restaurants throughout New Jersey and eastern Pennsylvania, conducted before and after the increase in the New Jersey minimum wage. Relative to restaurants in Pennsylvania, where the minimum wage remained unchanged, we find that employment in New Jersey actually *expanded* with the increase in the minimum wage. Furthermore, when we examine

---

16. Some of their discussion suggests they are interested in reopening some of the issues in a spirited methodological debate that took place almost fifty years ago among economists Richard Lester (1946, 1947), Fritz Machlup (1946, 1947), and George Stigler (1946, 1947).

17. Ibid., pp. 2–3.

18. Ibid., pp. 1–2, authors' emphasis.

restaurants within New Jersey, we find that employment was *higher* at restaurants that were forced to increase their wages to comply with the law than at those stores that already were paying more than the new minimum. We find similar results in studies of fast-food restaurants in Texas after the 1991 increase in the federal minimum wage and of teenage workers after the 1988 increase in California's minimum wage.

Second, a cross state analysis finds that the 1990 and 1991 increases in the federal minimum wage did not affect teenage employment adversely. The federal minimum increased from $3.35 per hour to $3.80 on April 1, 1990, and to $4.25 per hour on April 1, 1991. We categorized states into groups on the basis of the fraction of teenage workers who were earning between $3.35 and $3.80 per hour just before the first minimum-wage increase took effect. In high-wage states, such as California and Massachusetts, relatively few teenagers were in the range in which the minimum-wage increase would affect pay rates, whereas in low-wage states, such as Mississippi and Alabama, as many as 50 percent of teenagers were in the affected wage range. On the basis of the textbook model of the minimum wage, one would expect teenage employment to decrease in the low-wage states, where the federal minimum wage raised pay rates, relative to high-wage states, where the minimum had far less effect. Contrary to this expectation, our results show no meaningful difference in employment growth between high-wage and low-wage states. If anything, the states with the largest fraction of workers affected by the minimum wage had the largest gains in teenage employment. This conclusion continues to hold when we adjust for differences in regional economic growth that occurred during the early 1990s, and conduct the analysis with state-level data, rather than regional data. A similar analysis of employment trends for a broader sample of low-wage workers, and for employees in the retail trade and restaurant industries, likewise fails to uncover a negative employment effect of the federal minimum wage.

3

Examining the Evidence on Minimum Wages and Employment

Donald R. Deere, Kevin M. Murphy, and Finis R. Welch

Beginning about forty years ago there was a revolution in labor economics; what was once labor became economics. Instead of concentrating on the complexities and idiosyncracies of labor, research concentrated instead on commonality. Ordinary, garden variety economics was applied to labor and much was learned, or so we thought. It can be tempting to make too much of theory—its flexibility often precludes prediction. But of the few predictions, the most robust is the law of demand: if the price of something is raised artificially, less will be bought. The "something" includes labor; there is no qualification. Even if you are not an economist, who has had to recite the law of demand a thousand times, you can understand this no-free-lunch principle. Despite this conventional wisdom, recent attention from the media, the government, and even professional economists has focused on the potential to increase the minimum wage with no resulting loss of employment.

Our renewed interest in the effects of a minimum wage was triggered by the anomalous findings and conclusions of David Card and Alan Krueger, as summarized in their book *Myth and Measurement: The New Economics of the Minimum Wage* (1995, 1). The authors begin:

This book presents a new body of evidence showing that recent minimum-wage increases have
not had the negative employment effects predicted by the textbook model. Some of the evidence points toward a *positive* effect of the
minimum wage on employment, most shows no
effect at all. Moreover, a reanalysis of previous
minimum-wage studies finds little support for
the prediction that minimum wages reduce employment. If accepted, our findings call into
question the standard model of the labor market
that has dominated economists' thinking for the
past half century. (emphasis in original)

Although Messrs. Card and Krueger may not agree,
we believe they should be flattered by our attention. By
and large, we take their results seriously and we ask
whether there are alternative interpretations to those they
present. Their work is empirical, and empirical research
is like hunting for needles of truth in haystacks of conflicting phenomena. Since the bulk of their findings
shows that nothing changes whenever the minimum wage
is raised, we could simply have dismissed their searches
as inept. Even more perniciously, because they repeatedly
return from their searches empty-handed, we could argue,
as they do in their "meta-analysis" of the prior literature
in *The American Economic Review* (1995), that their searches
were prejudged and, therefore, biased. Dog bites man is
less newsworthy than man bites dog, and an announce-
ment that water runs uphill will draw a bigger crowd than
one to the contrary.

In what follows we present a combination of ideas
and "facts" about minimum wages with which the advo-
cates of the "new research" must contend. We begin with
a discussion of four often misunderstood conceptual issues that frame the debate over minimum wages. This is
followed by a description and interpretation of the empirical evidence regarding the employment effects of the minimum wage.

Issues

We first discuss the implications of increasing the minimum wage for employment in a particular sector of the economy, such as a sample of fast-food restaurants, and consider the size of potential employment effects in relation to the variation we typically see in measures of employment. We then discuss conditions under which an increase in the minimum wage raises teenagers' income, who pays for the income transfers, and what comparisons are useful for judging the level of the minimum wage.

The Putative Employment Effects of Increasing the Minimum Wage. As we noted in the introduction, empirical research is made more difficult by an inability to "hold other things equal," as the textbook predictions require. In response, some researchers have attempted to use so-called "natural experiments" to assess the employment effects of minimum wages. There are two problems, one theoretical and the other empirical, with using this research approach to generalize about the effects of minimum wages on employment.

Two of the cornerstone studies in *Myth and Measurement* are derived from surveys conducted by the authors that focus narrowly on portions of the fast-food industry. While the data quality of the New Jersey study has been sharply criticized, and the Texas study has so few observations that no conclusions are possible, the fundamental flaw in the fast-food studies is that they could never pretend to serve as a basis for generalization.

Nothing in economic theory implies that any particular subset of firms in a narrowly specified industry will be adversely affected by an increase in the minimum wage. Obviously an employer might applaud an increase in the minimum if it raises his competitors' costs more than his. If smaller firms are unskilled-labor-intensive, an increase in the minimum wage raises the cost of unskilled labor and, therefore, increases average firm size. Thus studies of existing firms might show increased employment, even though a higher minimum retards entry by firms that otherwise would have entered and reduces industrywide employment. Similarly, among fast-food businesses there are different kinds of restaurants that depend differently on low-wage labor. An increase in the minimum might increase costs more in Chinese and Mexican restaurants, causing consumers to substitute in favor of hamburgers. Studies of hamburger providers might show opposite effects of an increased minimum from studies of Chinese or Mexican restaurants.

Whether or not one is surprised by the finding that employment in surveyed fast-food restaurants in New Jersey increased relative to employment in surveyed fast-food restaurants in Pennsylvania, this is simply not informative about the generalized effect of minimum wages on employment.

In addition to squaring the empirical test with the theoretical prediction, it is important to employ tests with sufficient power to sort out the conflicting influences. The 1990–1991 increase in the minimum wage actually had a fairly small effect on labor costs, and measured employment varies substantially even when the minimum wage does not. In this kind of world—of experiments with small "treatments" and noisy "outcomes"—finding no effect or an occasional perverse effect is common.

Although the nominal minimum wage increased almost 27 percent in two steps from March 1990 to April 1991, a careful look at the data shows that the higher minimum increased the average cost of employing teenagers by less than 4 percent. The relatively small effect on labor cost implies that isolating the associated employment losses cannot be done haphazardly. The data also show, however, that had the federal minimum been raised to $4.25 at a much earlier date, as many then wanted, or if the minimum were to be increased to $5.15, as will hap-

FIGURE 3–1
ESTIMATED EFFECT ON AVERAGE WAGE COSTS OF INCREASING THE MINIMUM WAGE, FOR SIXTEEN THROUGH NINETEEN-YEAR-OLDS, 1979–1994
(percent change in average wage)

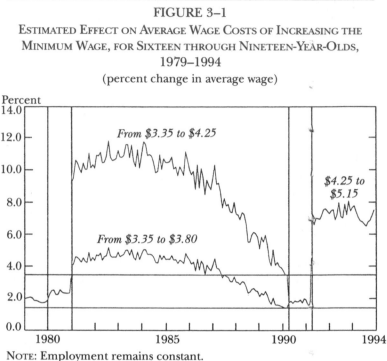

NOTE: Employment remains constant.
SOURCE: Authors' calculation.

pen in 1997, labor costs would rise two to three times as much.

We examine how increases in the federal minimum wage between 1979 and 1993 affected labor cost. The cost of a higher minimum is calculated before its introduction by taking everyone earning a wage between the existing minimum and the higher minimum and (hypothetically) raising the wage to the new minimum. The implied percentage increase in the average wage gives an estimate of the labor cost of the proposed higher minimum, assuming no employment loss.

Figure 3–1 presents these cost calculations on a month-by-month basis from 1979 through 1993 using teenagers (aged sixteen–nineteen) paid hourly in the

Current Population Survey outgoing rotation files. For each month, the chart gives the percentage increase in the average wage if the minimum wage were raised from its current level to the next level attained; the vertical lines denote when a new federal minimum actually took effect. For example, the minimum was raised to $3.35 on January 1, 1981. The next minimums are $3.80, which took effect April 1, 1990, and then $4.25, effective April 1, 1991. If the minimum had been raised from $3.35 to $3.80 in January 1981 instead, the average cost of teenage labor would have increased by about 4 percent. If the increase had been from $3.35 to $4.25 in January 1981, teenage labor costs would have increased by about 9 percent. Although these hypothetical increases of $.45 or $.90 would have increased the minimum wage by 13 percent or 27 percent, they would actually have raised the average teenage wage (assuming no employment loss) by only 4 percent and 9 percent, respectively.

Over time, as nominal wages drift upward, of course, the implied cost increase begins to shrink. By the time we get to the month before April 1, 1990, the estimated cost increases of going from $3.35 to either $3.80 or $4.25 are, as the horizontal lines indicate, less than 2 percent and 4 percent, respectively. This is the effect that must be detected when changes in teenage employment are examined. For example, suppose that the labor demand elasticity is −1 and that the teenage employment rate is 45 percent before April 1990; then the increase in the minimum from $3.35 to $4.25 would have reduced teenage employment by about 1.6 percentage points.

Figure 3–1 demonstrates vividly that the same percentage increase in the level of the minimum can have very different effects on the cost of teenage labor, depending on the actual distribution of teenage wages at the time of the increase. Minimum wage studies that merely rephrase the old adage, "a 10 percent increase in the minimum leads to an X percent decrease in teenage employment," ignore the true effect on labor costs.

Figure 3–1 is extended beyond April 1, 1991, in order to provide cost estimates of a further increase in the minimum wage to $5.15, as proposed by the Clinton administration and agreed to by Congress. Such an increase would have a much larger effect on teenage labor costs than any of the increases instituted since 1979. By the end of 1993, moving to a $5.15 minimum would have raised the average cost of employing teenagers by more than 7 percent. This cost increase is large because there has been relatively little upward movement in nominal teenage wages from the current $4.25 minimum; more than half of employed teenagers are earning between $4.25 and $5.15.

In addition to the limitations of a small cost effect from the 1990–1991 minimum-wage increase, the analysis of employment effects must contend with all the other things that affect measured employment rates. Differences in state or regional economies make it difficult to hold "all else" equal while noise in the data collection process renders estimates less precise. Systematic differences in state labor markets can obviously bias cross-state comparisons of employment as measures of minimum wage effects, and the "noise" from random sampling error makes it difficult to isolate the employment declines that result from higher minimum wages.

Observations on teenage employment rates move around quite a bit from month to month or quarter to quarter, because of random noise. After controlling for seasonal swings and the business cycle, the standard deviation of changes in state teenage employment rates in the outgoing rotation files ranges from 5.3 to 21.8 percentage points for changes from one month to the next, and from 3.5 to 11.8 percentage points for changes from one quarter to the next.

All this noise in period-to-period employment changes implies that searching for minimum-wage effects by simply comparing monthly or quarterly state employment rates before and after an increase in the minimum is futile. The minimum-wage increase would have to reduce teenage employment by about 20 percent (9 percentage points) in the least volatile, or largest states, or by about 80 percent (36 percentage points) in the most volatile, or smallest states, for there to be at least a 95 percent chance of observing a decline in employment. With smaller employment reductions, the chances of observing no change in employment or even an employment increase are substantial. Needless to say, a difference-in-differences approach that compares the change in one state's employment with the change in another only compounds the difficulty.

The Minimum Wage and Teenage Income. It has been observed that much of the pre-1990s research on the minimum wage centered around the finding that a 10 percent increase in the minimum wage results in a less than 10 percent reduction in teenage employment. In fact, in their oft-quoted review of the literature, Brown, Gilroy, and Kohen (1982) found that most studies suggest that a 10 percent increase in the minimum wage results in a 1 percent to 3 percent decline in teenage employment, and the authors state that the lower end of this range is probably most accurate. Citing this result, a number of economists support increased minimums.[1] The argument is that

---

1. In the 1995 and 1996 meetings of the American Economics Association there was a session devoted to the minimum wage. In the 1995 session, Charles Brown, in his discussion of the papers, stated that provided teenage unemployment spells were relatively short, which he believed to be true, the finding that teenage employment fell by a smaller percentage than the increase in the minimum wage led him to support an increase in the minimum. In the 1996 session, Richard B. Freeman, in his presentation, stated that one of the things you would want to know before supporting an increased minimum was whether the minimum wage rose by a greater percentage than the drop in teenage employment. Citing the above result from Brown, Gilroy, and Kohen, he then stated his support for an increased minimum.

the income gain among teenagers remaining employed because of the increased minimum is greater than the income loss due to lost employment. The implication is that despite the employment losses, increased minimums have a net positive effect on total teen income. This argument is wrongheaded on several counts.

First, and most obvious, a 10 percent increase in the minimum does not represent a 10 percent increase in the wage of all teenagers. A majority of teenagers already earns above the new minimum wage, even before it is increased. For example, when the minimum was last increased from $3.35 to $4.25 in 1990 and 1991, a 27 percent increase, the average cost of employing teenagers increased by about 4 percent, assuming no employment loss and full compliance with the new law. The logic of the proponents' argument, described above, is that unless the 27 percent increase in the minimum resulted in a 27 percent reduction in teenage employment, teenage income would increase. While you might agree that this argument would be cold comfort to the job losers, you can also see that it is simply wrong. Since the ex ante calculated wage (labor cost) increase is only 4 percent—1.5 percent for each 10 percent increase in the minimum—you would immediately adjust the compensating employment loss from 27 percent to 4 percent. But this would also be too much, because the job losers are those who, in the absence of the increased minimum, earned the least, and the net employment loss (4 percent) is smaller than the gross employment loss.

The 4 percent increase in ex ante teen wage cost was calculated assuming no employment loss and full compliance with the new $4.25 minimum. When the minimum was increased from $3.35 to $4.25, all teens earning $3.35 to $4.24 were in line to receive a raise. For example, teens earning the previous minimum of $3.35 were in line for a 90 cent increase, while teens earning $4.20 were in line for a 5 cent increase. Assuming that all the teens who were in line for a raise actually got one, and averaging these raises with the zero raises for those already earning at least $4.25, gives the calculated 4 percent average wage increase. But the employment losses that occur, as well as any noncompliance, are not distributed evenly among teenagers. (Appendix 3–A contains an example that analyzes the distribution of employment losses and wage gains among those workers earning below the new minimum.) Clearly, no teens already earning $4.25 or more lost jobs because of the new law. Among those teens earning less than $4.25, where employment was lost, job losses were most likely for exactly those teens who were slated for the biggest raises. The 4 percent ex ante calculation of increased teen wages overstates the actual increase in teen income because job losses and noncompliance were concentrated among those who would have received the largest wage increases.

The observed employment decline among teens when the minimum went from $3.35 to $4.25 represents only the net effect of teens previously out of the labor force taking jobs and teens previously employed losing jobs. By their choice not to work at the $3.35 minimum, teens previously out of the labor force have shown the value of their time out of the market to be greater than $3.35. If one of these teens takes a job at the $4.25 minimum, thereby displacing a teen who was earning $3.35, then the actual increase in income is less than the 90 cent increase in the wage. The greater is the gross change in teen employment relative to the net employment change the more the observed change in average teen wages overstates the actual increase in teen income.

Finally, there is the source of the "10 percent increase in the minimum causes a 1 percent to 3 percent decline in teenage employment" conventional wisdom. This estimate is derived by comparing movements in teenage employment over time, and perhaps across industries, to movements in the minimum wage deflated by an average wage. This measure of the relative minimum wage is meant to gauge the fraction of employment affected by the minimum. The minimum wage has its effects on workers who earn, or would earn, low wages, and not on those at the average wage. The accuracy of using an average wage as a deflator depends on the relationship between low wages and the average wage. As documented by recent research, the gap between the average wage and low wages is not fixed but has expanded substantially in recent years. Deflating the nominal minimum by the average wage necessarily must measure effective changes in the minimum wage with error. As a result the estimates of the effect of the minimum wage on teenage employment will be biased and will understate the true effect. The recent finding that the time-series estimates of minimum-wage employment effects decline when data from the 1980s are included may be nothing more than increased measurement error in the minimum wage variable.

The Minimum Wage as a Transfer Program. Most of the minimum-wage literature tries to measure the net employment effect of increasing the minimum wage. Absent employment losses, the minimum wage would just be a program that transfers money from one group, those who buy the fruits of low-wage labor, to a different group, the low-wage workers.

Does such a transfer program make sense? A higher minimum wage essentially takes money from the people in front of the counter at McDonald's and gives it to the people behind the counter. At first glance, these two groups of people appear similar. About one-third of those earning the minimum wage are teenagers, most of whom will outgrow being low-wage workers and many of whom are not in poor families. Those on the buying side include the nonworking poor (and most of the poor do not work). These individuals are not helped by a higher minimum wage they do not get, but they are harmed by higher prices.

The employment reductions that come from imposing or raising a minimum wage only make matters worse.
Not only is the pie smaller, but there is also a perverse
redistribution among workers. Those workers who are
least-skilled are priced out of the labor market, while the
somewhat higher-skilled remain employed and receive
the wage increase. Moreover, much of the redistribution
that occurs as low-skill workers are replaced by more-
skilled workers is not visible in the aggregate data because
estimated employment effects capture only the net
change in employment. There may be many more people
displaced when the minimum rises than there are total
jobs lost.

Measuring the Value of the Minimum Wage. The claim is
often made in support of increasing the minimum wage
that its value has fallen to a forty, or more, year low. While
the federal minimum relative to the consumer price index
(CPI) is low by historical standards, this is not a useful
comparison. In thinking about the minimum wage as a
source of income we should compare it to other income
sources, particularly wages. In thinking about the minimum wage as the price of labor, obviously we should compare it to other wages. The relative decline of wages
during the past two to three decades for those paid below
the median wage has received quite a bit of attention. Yet
this fact is ignored when the downward path of the "real"
minimum wage is measured. Adding to this the well-
known flaws in the CPI, both current and especially historical, that cause it to overstate increases in the cost of living,
particularly during the 1970s, implies that comparing the
minimum wage to other wages provides the correct measure of its effect.

Figure 3–2 provides information on the federal minimum wage relative to the value of other wages. The figure
shows how the minimum compares with the wages of
twenty-five to thirty-four-year olds who are paid by the

FIGURE 3–2

MINIMUM WAGE RELATIVE TO WAGE MEASURES FOR WORKERS
TWENTY-FIVE THROUGH THIRTY-FOUR YEARS OLD, 1979–1994

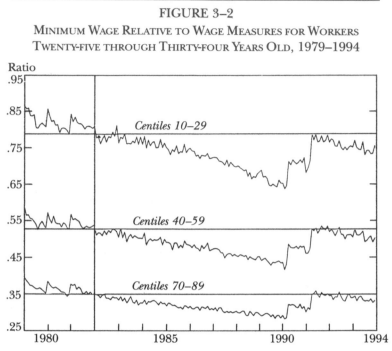

SOURCE: Authors' calculations.

hour. Except for the very lowest earners, this age group should be unaffected by changes in the minimum wage. Using the outgoing rotation files of the Current Population Survey for each month we first computed the wage at each percentile of the hourly wage distribution for twenty-five to thirty-four-year-olds and then averaged these wage values for the tenth through twenty-ninth, fortieth through fifty-ninth, and seventieth through eighty-ninth percentiles, respectively. These average percentiles represent the first quintile, the median, and the fourth quintile of wages for twenty-five to thirty-four-year-olds. The figure plots the value of the federal minimum wage relative to the averaged percentile values for each month from 1979 to 1993.

There was clear erosion in the relative minimum

38

wage during the long period in which the federal minimum remained at $3.35. Not coincidentally, according to the 1996 *Economic Report of the President*, teenage employment rates rose sharply during this same period (1981–1989). The relative minimum then increased in two steps during 1990 and 1991 as the federal minimum was raised to $3.80 and then to $4.25. The three horizontal lines in the figure mark the level of the relative minimum just after it was raised to $4.25 on April 1, 1991, while the vertical line denotes December 31, 1981. By historical standards of the 1980s, the minimum wage at the end of 1993 is not particularly low; it is at about the level of 1982 or 1983.

Evidence

We first take another look at employment trends for teenagers in New Jersey and Pennsylvania and in Puerto Rico. We then briefly review evidence we developed earlier on employment effects at the beginning of the 1990s, and we present new evidence on employment effects for the minimum wage increases put into effect in both 1980–1981 and 1990–1991.

New Jersey and Pennsylvania. The minimum wage study that has received by far the most attention was based on a survey of fast-food providers in New Jersey and Pennsylvania around April 1, 1992, when New Jersey increased its minimum wage to $5.05. President Clinton even cited this study in his 1995 State of the Union Address when he called for an increase in the federal minimum to $5.15. While we have already mentioned the fast-food studies, it is instructive to examine what happened to teenage employment statewide in New Jersey and Pennsylvania. Figure 3–3 plots employment rates for teenage males in these two states and the entire United States. Employment in New Jersey diverges from Pennsylvania's and the rest of

39

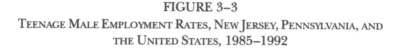

FIGURE 3-3

TEENAGE MALE EMPLOYMENT RATES, NEW JERSEY, PENNSYLVANIA, AND
THE UNITED STATES, 1985–1992

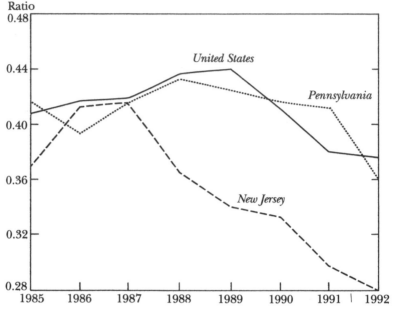

SOURCE: Authors' calculations.

the country's, beginning in 1988. At the time of the increase in New Jersey's minimum wage on April 1, 1992,
however, the employment rate in both states falls, though
it does fall by less in New Jersey. This relative increase in
New Jersey employment seems a thin reed on which to
build a case for positive employment effects of the minimum wage.

Puerto Rico. The "problem" of small changes in the minimum wage has plagued much of the research on minimum wages. One response has been to look for cases
where the effect of minimum wages on labor cost is particularly large—for example, Puerto Rico. Beginning in 1974

40

FIGURE 3-4

EMPLOYMENT AND THE KAITZ INDEX FOR PUERTO RICO, 1950–1985

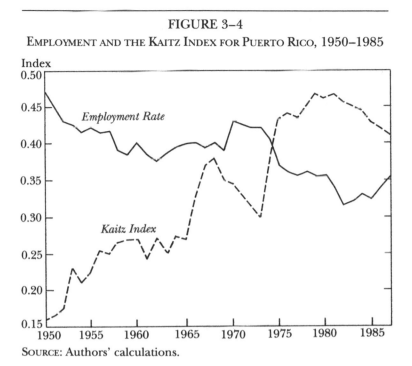

SOURCE: Authors' calculations.

the level and coverage of the minimum wage in Puerto Rico were raised to match the U.S. standard. By 1983, Puerto Rico had the same minimum, $3.35, and the same extent of coverage as the mainland.

Figure 3-4 plots the Puerto Rican annual employment rate and the Kaitz index of the (relative) minimum wage in Puerto Rico. Figure 3-4 shows a strong relationship between employment and the minimum-wage index; as the minimum rises employment falls, and as the minimum falls employment rises. One look at this picture makes it difficult to conclude that minimum wages do not reduce employment. A simple regression of the employment rate on the Kaitz index gives a coefficient of −.32 (equivalent to a simple correlation of −.82) and a t-statistic of −8.7. An employment rate regression that also controls for trend and the U.S. unemployment rate and that covers only the 1974–1987 period when the minimum was increased to the U.S. level gives a coefficient of $-.35$ on the Kaitz index, with a t-statistic of -3.6. Note that the employment rate refers to total employment on the island and not just teenage employment. Finally, we note that Castillo-Freeman and Freeman (1992) conclude that "migration has been a key 'safety valve' in the Puerto Rican job market without which it would have been virtually impossible to impose the U.S.-level minimum on the island." A sobering thought for those in the United States displaced by a higher minimum wage!

Previous Research. In addition to the fast-food studies, the other two cornerstone studies of *Myth and Measurement* examine teenage employment and minimum wages across states. California raised its minimum wage from $3.35 to $4.25 effective July 1, 1988. *Myth and Measurement* compares the changes in employment in California with changes in employment in a collection of other locales where the minimum did not increase and finds that teenage employment rose in California relative to the other places. *Myth and Measurement* also makes a cross-state comparison of teenage employment to examine the effects of the increase in the federal minimum from $3.35 to $3.80 on April 1, 1990. Here the idea is that the minimum wage increase will result in a larger employment decline in states where a greater fraction of teenagers earn low wages, as compared with states with teens earning higher wages. The study finds, however, that teenage employment fell in high-wage states relative to low-wage states.

While it is tempting to think that low-wage states will suffer greater employment losses from an increase in the minimum wage because the effect on labor cost is greater, this may not be correct. It is not the effect on labor cost per se that reduces employment—rather it is the availability of substitutes when these costs rise. A state with few low-wage workers has relatively many higher-wage workers ready to step in and take the place of a worker who is priced out of the market. In contrast, a state with many low-wage workers has fewer alternatives; the cost of potential substitutes has also gone up as the minimum wage rises. As an extreme example, a state with only low-wage workers cannot substitute for better workers; hence employment will fall only as capital can be substituted for labor or as scale effects take hold. Thus the conceptual experiment of comparing employment changes and initial wage levels across states does not necessarily identify the effect of minimum wages on low-wage workers.

Ignoring this caveat, we also compare changes in the employment rates of low- and high-wage populations. In previous research we note that grouping workers by state is only one of several ways to conduct this comparison. We use the Current Population Survey outgoing rotation data to partition workers into low- and high-wage populations in seven ways: based on age, education, race, ethnicity, marital status, and gender, in addition to state of residence. Within each partition we compare employment changes (calculated from the twelve months prior to the April 1, 1990, minimum increase to the twelve months after the April 1, 1991, increase) to the fraction of workers earning less than $4.25 in the twelve months prior to April 1, 1990.

Table 3–1 lists the employment changes alongside the incidence of low wages for the indicated groups. The incidence of low wages and the employment changes are reported separately for men and women. The age comparisons show that employment declines are greatest for teenagers followed by young adults, two of the groups with the highest proportions with low wages. The comparisons based on race and ethnicity as well as the comparisons by education and marital status show a strong positive relationship between the incidence of low wages and the subsequent employment decline. The only exceptions are that employment fell less for women than for men and

TABLE 3–1
FRACTION OF LOW-WAGE WORKERS AND THE PERCENTAGE
CHANGE IN EMPLOYMENT-POPULATION RATIOS OVER LEVELS FOR
APRIL 1, 1989–MARCH 31, 1990, BY SELECTED
POPULATION CHARACTERISTICS

Group	Men		Women	
	Fraction low wage	Employment change twelve months beginning April 1, 1991	Fraction low wage	Employment change twelve months beginning April 1, 1991
Age				
15–19	44.5	−15.4	51.8	−12.9
20–24	14.2	−5.6	19.0	−4.3
25–64	3.3	−2.5	8.8	−0.3
65–69	14.0	−4.3	21.0	3.5
Race				
Black	11.0	−4.8	16.9	−3.4
White	7.2	−3.1	13.0	−0.6
Asian	5.4	0.7	9.3	−0.3
Spanish ethnicity				
Mexican	15.6	−4.8	21.9	−5.5
Other Spanish	8.8	−3.3	16.4	−0.7
Non-Spanish	7.1	−3.2	12.9	−0.8
Years of school completed				
<12	20.7	−6.6	35.4	−7.3
12	6.0	−4.0	13.5	−2.2
>12	3.5	−2.8	6.4	−0.7
Marital status				
Single	15.1	−4.4	18.4	−3.2
Married	2.7	−2.4	9.0	0.7
States				
10 Lowest	13.1	−1.5	23.7	0.0
Middle	7.9	−3.4	14.2	−0.7
10 Highest	3.5	−4.0	5.6	−2.9
All	7.5	−3.2	13.3	−1.1

NOTE: Single refers to all but married, spouse present.
SOURCE: Authors' calculations.

FIGURE 3–5

CHANGES IN EMPLOYMENT RATES FOR MALES TWENTY-FIVE TO FIFTY-FOUR, WITH MORE THAN TWELVE YEARS OF EDUCATION, 1989–1992

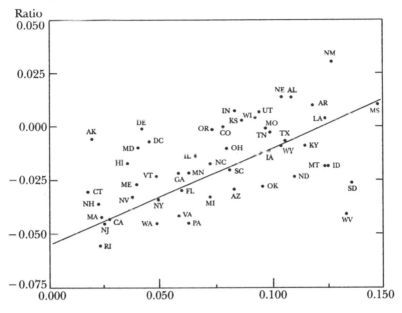

SOURCE: Authors' calculations.

that employment fell less in states with a high incidence of low-wage workers. The former finding can be easily explained by the long-term trend of increasing employment for women relative to men.

The state results may seem anomalous, but they are likely to reflect the fact that employment growth has been greater in states with lower wages. To illustrate, figure 3–5 graphs the change in employment between 1989 and 1992 for men aged twenty-five to fifty-four with at least thirteen years of education (a group unaffected by the minimum wage) against the fraction of all men in the state with low wages. The relationship is strong and positive (the fitted regression line in the figure has a t ratio of 7.8). As is true for gender, the underlying trend of relatively more rapid

45

growth in low-wage states is not reversed by the increase in the federal minimum wage. We do not view our gender and state findings as refutation of the law of demand; instead we take them as a warning that minimum wages are not everything that affects employment and that other things must be considered before one can correctly assess the employment effects of minimum wages.

The results in table 3–1 suggest a strong relationship between changes in employment around the 1990–1991 minimum-wage increase and the incidence of low wages. Other changes in the economy, such as the falling aggregate employment during the recession, may account for part of these findings. In table 3–2 we use regression to adjust for changes in aggregate employment and examine the remaining changes in employment for six groups that have relatively high concentrations of low-wage workers. Table 3–2 is organized by gender and race, with teenagers (aged fifteen–nineteen) in the upper panel and adult (aged twenty–fifty-four) high school dropouts in the lower panel. The first column refers to men of all races, the second column to women of all races, and the third column to blacks, both men and women. The numbers in the table are estimates of the percentage loss in employment for each group from the 1990–1991 increase in the minimum wage net of the expected employment losses attributable to movements in aggregate employment.

These estimates show that the employment of young workers and workers with little education is quite sensitive to the minimum wage. Teenage employment dropped sharply following the 1990 increase in the federal minimum and dropped again after the second increase in 1991. Compared with the employment level projected had the federal minimum remained at \$3.35, teenage employment was 4.8 percent, 6.6 percent, and 7.5 percent lower in 1990 for men, women, and blacks, respectively, and 7.3 percent, 11.4 percent, and 10.0 percent lower in 1991–

TABLE 3–2
ESTIMATES OF EMPLOYMENT LOSSES FROM THE 1990–1991
INCREASE IN THE FEDERAL MINIMUM WAGE
(percent)

Increase	Teenagers, 15–19		
($)	Men	Women	Blacks
3.35 to 3.80	–4.8	–6.6	–7.8
3.35 to 4.25	–7.3	–11.4	–10.0

Increase	High School Dropouts, Adults 20–54		
($)	Men	Women	Blacks
3.35 to 3.80	–1.5	–2.5	–4.4
3.35 to 4.25	–3.1	–5.2	–6.7

SOURCE: Authors' calculations.

1992. The estimates for adult high school dropouts also show a decline in employment following the increase in the minimum to $3.80, and a further decline after the increase to $4.25. Compared with the expected employment level projected maintaining a $3.35 federal minimum, employment of adult high school dropouts was 1.5 percent, 2.5 percent, and 4.4 percent lower in 1990 for men, women, and blacks, respectively, and 3.1 percent, 5.2 percent, and 6.7 percent lower in 1991–1992.

While these results show that the minimum-wage effects for teenagers are large because of their disproportionate representation among low-wage workers, they also show significant negative employment effects of the minimum wage for adults with little education. Teenagers make up a significant part of the low-wage population, but they are not a majority. Only 32 percent of those with low wages just before the 1990 increase in the federal minimum were aged fifteen–nineteen, while 20 percent were of Spanish ethnicity, 16 percent were black, and 12 percent were women over the age of nineteen with fewer than twelve years of schooling. Teenagers bear a significant part of the burden from minimum wages, but most will outgrow it. The remaining two-thirds of the low-wage population, which is disproportionately minority, female, and poorly educated, is less likely to be so lucky.

New Results. An analysis using outgoing rotation files from 1979–1993 provides strong evidence that minimum wages reduce employment. Figure 3–6 plots the employment and wages of teenagers (aged sixteen–nineteen) relative to that of twenty–twenty-four-year-olds. The data are based on national averages for each month from 1979 through 1993. In each figure the four vertical lines mark the occasion of an increase in the federal minimum wage. Panel A shows the teenage employment-to-population ratio relative to the employment-to-population ratio of young adults. After bottoming out in 1983, there is a steady rise in teenage employment up through 1989—just before the minimum wage is increased. Panel D plots teenage wages relative to young adult wages averaged around the twentieth percentile in each wage distribution. From 1984 through 1989 teenage wages fell, but they then increased sharply as the minimum wage was increased to $4.25 during 1990–1991. Comparing the patterns in these two graphs shows that teenage employment and wages move in opposite directions, and that movements in teenage wages are driven by the minimum wage. Controlling for seasonal effects and for a time trend, the elasticity of the relative teenage employment rate with respect to relative teenage wages is −0.68 with a *t*-statistic of −11.2 (as reported in the figure).

The remaining two graphs plot different measures of teenage employment relative to the analogous employment measure for young adults. Panel B plots the (relative) employment of those paid by the hour as a fraction of the total population. The pattern here is the same as for all employment, while the swings are even more pronounced. Controlling for seasonality and trend, the elasticity of the relative teenage hourly employment rate with respect to relative teenage wages is − 0.98, with a *t*-statistic of − 12.1. Panel C plots the (relative) fraction of employment that is paid by the hour. Though these data are more noisy, there is an unmistakable pattern that matches the other employment series. Controlling for seasonality and trend, the elasticity of the relative share of teenage employment that is paid by the hour with respect to relative teenage wages is − 0.30 with a *t*-statistic of − 6.1. These two graphs suggest that there are other forms of substitution in response to minimum wages. As the minimum wage increases fewer teenagers are employed, while those who remained employed move away from being paid by the hour toward jobs with other forms of compensation, such as piece rates for lawn mowing, where enforcement of the minimum wage is more difficult.

The lesson of figure 3–6 is that teenage employment is significantly affected by the minimum wage. Not only does employment fall as minimum wages rise, but the composition of employment shifts away from those paid by the hour. The effects on employment were understandably largest following the 1990–1991 hike in the minimum wage, but there is also a clear increase in teenage employment as the minimum wage erodes during the mid–1980s.

Conclusions

This look at the data provides ample support for the notion that the law of demand remains intact—an artificial increase in the price of something, including labor, causes less of it to be bought. We have also found clues to suggest why some researchers have been unable to isolate negative minimum-wage effects. Not only is there clear evidence

FIGURE 3–6
Employment and Wage Ratios for Teenagers Aged Sixteen through Nineteen Relative to Youths Aged Twenty through Twenty-four, 1979–1993

Employment / Population
Wage elasticity = −0.68 ($t=$ −11.2)

A. Standard deviation units

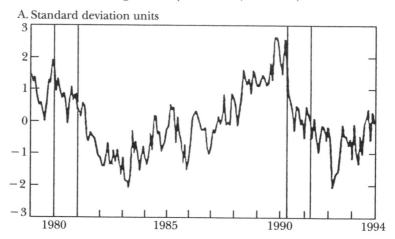

Paid Hourly Employment / Total Employment
Wage Elasticity = −0.30 ($t=$ −6.1)

C. Standard deviation units

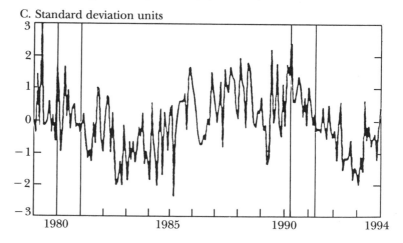

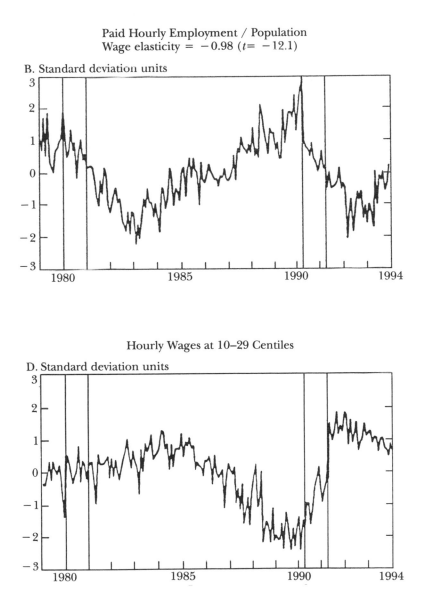

Paid Hourly Employment / Population
Wage elasticity = − 0.98 (t= − 12.1)

B. Standard deviation units

Hourly Wages at 10–29 Centiles

D. Standard deviation units

SOURCE: Authors' calculations.

that past minimum wage increases have reduced employment, particularly among teenagers, but the signs also suggest that a further increase in the minimum to $5.15
would have a much greater impact on teenage labor cost,
and thus on teenage employment, than any of the recent
increases. First, the 27 percent increase in the nominal
minimum wage during 1990–1991 increased average teenage wages by less than 4 percent, because most teenagers
were already earning $4.25 or more. Second, baseline em-
ployment levels are difficult to hold constant because of
systematic differences in employment across states and
randomness in the data collection process through time.
Third, in Puerto Rico, where the effect of minimum wages
on labor cost is more pronounced, much of the baby is
thrown out with bath water in correcting for serial correlation and common trends and in "spreading" the minimum wage variable across several leads and lags. The
small cost effect of the 1990–1991 minimum-wage increase coupled with the volatility of employment implies
that researchers must bring sufficient data to bear on the
question to give their tests power.

Finally, we have argued that even if one is willing to
overlook the employment losses by low-skill workers from
a higher minimum wage, such a policy makes little sense
on distributional grounds. It is far from clear that the buy-
ers of the fruits of low-wage labor are any better off than
are the workers, while it is clear that many low-wage workers are not from low-income families.

Appendix 3–A

This example is intended to amplify (part of) the fallacy
of the "unit elasticity" argument favoring increases in the
minimum wage. Suppose that the minimum wage is increased from $3.35 to $4.25 per hour, as in the 1990–1991
period, and that the ex ante calculation of the wage cost
increase is 4 percent, while the *observed* loss in employ-

ment is also 4 percent. Did teenage income remain unchanged?

In this example we ignore cross-effects where the demand for those previously earning more than $4.25 per hour increases and their nonparticipant counterparts are perhaps drawn into the market. We also ignore the potential supply responses of those who otherwise would earn less than $4.25 whose reservation wage, while below $4.25, exceeds their offer wage. Each of these responses tends to shift the composition of employment among heterogeneous teenagers in favor of those who, in the absence of mandated wage floors, have the greatest earning potential.

To keep things close to "the facts," assume that among those earning from $3.35 to $4.25 before the increase, one-half earn $3.35 exactly, while the remaining one-half are continuously distributed over the $3.35–$4.25 interval with a triangular density, beginning with zero mass at $3.35 and proceeding linearly thereafter.

The average wage of those earning above $3.35, but below $4.25, lies two-thirds of the way between $3.35 and $4.25, which is $3.95; so the combined average of those at $3.35 and those between $3.35 and $4.25 is $3.65 per hour. Without employment effects, the average wage of this group increases to $4.25, or by approximately 16.4 percent. So if the total increase is 4 percent, then the sub-$4.25 workers must account for roughly one-quarter of the teenage population.

Now consider those individuals whose ex ante wage is $3.35 + x$, where $0 \leq x \leq \$0.90$. Suppose that the probability that such individuals will lose their jobs following an increase in the minimum is exactly proportionate to the percentage cost increase that is imposed by the higher minimum. With factor η, the probability is

$\eta(\frac{.9 - x}{3.35 + x})$, and its complement, the probability of remaining employed, is

$1 - \eta(\frac{.9 - x}{3.35 + x})$. Since the wage gain, with retained employment, is $.9 - x$, and the wage loss for job losers is $3.35 + x$, the expected gain is

$$[1 - \eta(\frac{.9 - x}{3.35 + x})](.9 - x) - \eta(\frac{.9 - x}{3.35 + x})(3.35 + x) =$$

$$(.9 - x)[1 - \eta(\frac{4.25}{3.35 + x})] = G(x)$$

Interestingly, if $\eta \geqslant 1$, the expected gain is negative at all x. Moreover, since

$G'(x) \propto 4.25^2\eta - (3.35 + x)^2$, with $\eta = 1$, the "gain" is everywhere increasing, that is, the loss is decreasing, in x.

Now to proceed with the example, a 4 percent ex ante wage-cost increase against a 4 percent employment loss, the value of the factor of proportionality becomes $\eta = 0.945$.[2] This value for η implies that only those previously earning above $4.01 will gain. The maximum average gain in this case (at an ex ante wage of $4.13) is $0.003 per hour and the maximum loss (at an ex ante wage of $3.35) is $0.18 per hour.

---

2. The density of x is as described above as the proportion of teenagers that is directly affected. All that remains is to integrate the employment loss in (1), above, over the x-density, and to solve the one remaining equation for η.

4

Reconciling the Evidence on Employment Effects of Minimum Wages—A Review of Our Research Findings

David Neumark and William Wascher

O ur research on minimum wages now comprises seven works written over a period of five years. When we were in graduate school, the Minimum Wage Study Commission had recently completed a five-volume study of the employment effects of minimum-wage laws. The authors of the papers included in the study constituted a *Who's Who* in labor economics, and the breadth of the papers suggested that there was little more to be learned about this issue; indeed, for a number of years, new studies of the minimum wage were virtually nonexistent. Then, beginning in the late 1980s, a series of state-level increases in minimum wages were enacted, superseding the federal minimum of $3.35 (and later $4.25). Given the interest in regional variation in many other areas of labor economics, and given that nearly all the earlier work on minimum wages was based on time-

The views expressed are those of the authors only, and do not necessarily reflect those of the Federal Reserve Board or its staff. This chapter was prepared for the American Enterprise Institute conference "Employment and the Minimum Wage: An Examination and Critique of the Evidence from Empirical Research," June 1, 1995.

series evidence, it seemed fruitful to exploit the new state-level variation in minimum wages to reexamine evidence on the employment effects of minimum wages in low-wage labor markets.

In our first paper on this topic (Neumark and Wascher 1992), we used state-year observations from 1973 to 1989 to estimate minimum-wage effects from the type of employment regressions used in the existing time-series literature. For both teenagers (aged sixteen–nineteen) and young adults (aged sixteen–twenty-four), we concluded that most of the evidence indicated elasticities of employment with respect to minimum wages in the range −0.1 to −0.2, consistent with much of the earlier time-series evidence.[1] We also found that subminimum wages for youths moderated the disemployment effects of minimum wages.

We were not the only researchers to think of exploiting the increases in state minimum-wage rates in the late 1980s. David Card wrote two papers, one studying the increase in California's minimum wage in 1988 (Card 1992b), and another—very close in spirit to our paper—that exploited the variation in changes in the effective minimum wage across states associated with the increase in the federal minimum in 1990, at a time when state minimum wages varied greatly (Card 1992a). In contrast with our findings, Card concluded from the evidence in his papers that minimum-wage increases caused no adverse employment effects for teenagers. Later, in perhaps the most influential of the "revisionist" minimum-wage studies, Card and Alan Krueger (1994) found that employment at fast-food restaurants grew relatively faster in New Jersey than in Pennsylvania following the 1992 increase

---

1. Other papers in the recent round of research on minimum wages that found disemployment effects of minimum wages include Deere et al. (1995), Currie and Fallick (1993), Kim and Taylor (1995), and Williams (1993).

in the New Jersey minimum wage.[2] In addition, Card and Krueger, along with Lawrence Katz, wrote a detailed comment on our 1992 paper, claiming that "a corrected analysis of Neumark and Wascher's data shows that state-specific minimum wage increases during the 1970s and 1980s had no systematic effect on teenage employment" (Card et al. 1994, 496).

Given this array of evidence against the prediction that minimum wages reduce employment, it might have been the safest course to pack up our bags (or at least our computers) and turn our attention to other issues. As our reply to the Card et al. comment indicated, however, we were confident that we had gotten most of the answers right in our 1992 paper (Neumark and Wascher 1994a). More important, we found the revisionist results intriguing. Although the inconsistency of the revisionist minimum-wage studies with the competitive model of labor demand led some researchers to consider alternative theories of the low-wage labor market, we were of the opinion that empirical labor economists needed to conduct additional research before the new evidence on minimum wages could be embraced and the competitive model dismissed.[3]

Consequently, our subsequent research on minimum wages has focused on the data and empirical approaches used in the recent research, to attempt to uncover the sources of divergent results and, if possible, to arrive at a consistent picture of low-wage labor markets and the effects of minimum wages on the individuals in these markets. In our view, this research effort has met with some

---

2. That paper followed an earlier study by Katz and Krueger (1992) on the effect of the federal minimum wage increase in 1990 on the fast-food industry in Texas. Other papers in the recent round of research that found little or no effect of minimum wages on employment include Spriggs (1992) and Wellington (1991).

3. See Card and Krueger (1995, chapter 11), Rebitzer and Taylor (1991), Manning (1993), and Lang and Kahn (1995).

success. By extending the methods usually used to study employment effects of minimum wages to account for the possibility that minimum wages may be nonbinding in some markets, by accounting for the fact that the teenage group typically studied in research on minimum wages includes both higher- and lower-skilled workers, and by examining more carefully the data used in some of the existing research, we have reached the conclusion that the competitive model of low-wage labor markets and its prediction for the employment effects of minimum wages has not been contradicted by the revisionist evidence.[4]

In the following sections, we review the evidence that we have accumulated on the employment effects of minimum wages. We point out specific areas of agreement and of disagreement between our research and that of others, and, where possible, we offer our reconciliation of the conflicting results. As a review, this chapter gives short shrift to many of the issues discussed at length in the individual articles. We have tried to highlight, however, the central elements of our methods and our key results, and to provide a sense of the strength of the evidence.

The ILRR Symposium and Subsequent Exchange

The October 1992 issue of the *Industrial and Labor Relations Review* (ILRR) included a symposium containing three papers that used similar approaches to estimate the employment effects of minimum wages—two by Card and one by us. Our paper applied the standard model used in the time-series literature to state-level panel data on the fifty states and Washington, D.C., for the period 1973–1989. In particular, we estimated regressions of the form:

---

4. This contrasts with Card and Krueger's conclusion that their findings "pose a serious challenge to the simple textbook theory that economists have used to describe the effect of the minimum wage" (1995, 4).

$$E_{it} = \alpha MW_{it} + R_{it}\beta + \epsilon_{it} \qquad (4\text{--}1)$$

where E_{it} is the employment-to-population ratio for a particular demographic group, and R_{it} is a vector of control variables (including fixed state and year effects). MW_{it} is a coverage-adjusted relative minimum wage, constructed as federal coverage for the state, multiplied by the higher of the federal or state minimum-wage level, divided by the average wage in the state.

As long as changes in the minimum-wage variable are viewed as exogenous, α identifies the effect of minimum wages on employment. We estimated this equation for teenagers (sixteen–nineteen) and young adults (sixteen–twenty-four), and we reported results from a lengthy array of alternative specifications and estimators. Subsequent exchanges have focused on two particular specification issues: 1) whether to include a school enrollment rate among the control variables R_{it} (and how to measure it), and 2) the appropriate formulation and specification of the included minimum-wage variable. Panel A of table 4–1 summarizes the key results from our paper, reporting fixed-effects (within-group) estimates of the elasticity of employment with respect to minimum wages.

Three of the findings in panel A are most relevant to our subsequent research and to our attempts to reconcile the disparate research findings. First, a significant negative effect of minimum wages on employment of teenagers appears only in specifications that include the enrollment rate. Second, the estimated minimum-wage effects are stronger—both for teenagers and for young adults—when lagged minimum wages (of one year) are included. Third, in contrast to the results for teenagers, the estimated disemployment effect for sixteen–twenty-four-year-olds is largely invariant to the inclusion of the enrollment rate.

This combined evidence presents a puzzle. The simple textbook theory, in which workers (at least those of the same age) are homogeneous, would predict that mini-

TABLE 4–1
ESTIMATES OF ELASTICITIES OF EMPLOYMENT WITH RESPECT TO MINIMUM WAGES

Panel A: Basic Estimates

	Contemporaneous Minimum Wage, enrollment excluded	Add Enrollment Rate	Add Lagged Minimum Wage	Add Both
Teenagers, within-group	0.06	−0.14[a]	−0.03	−0.19[a]
Young adults, within-group	−0.07	−0.10[a]	−0.18[a]	−0.17[a]

Panel B: Alternative Enrollment Rate

	Contemporaneous Minimum Wage, enrollment excluded	Add Enrollment Rate	Add Lagged Minimum Wage	Add Both
Teenagers, within-group	N.A.	N.A.	N.A.	−0.11
Young adults, within-group	N.A.	N.A.	N.A.	−0.16[a]

Panel C: Instrument for Enrollment Rate

	Original Enrollment Rate	Alternative Enrollment Rate
Teenagers, within-group	−0.25[a]	−0.17
Young adults, within-group	−0.16[a]	−0.12[a]

Panel D: First Difference Estimates

	Contemporaneous Minimum Wage, enrollment excluded	Add Enrollment Rate	Add Lagged Minimum Wage	Add Both
Teenagers, one-year first difference	0.20	0.06	−0.12	−0.15
Young adults, one-year first difference	0.05	−0.01	−0.17	−0.19[b]

NOTES: Elasticities are evaluated at sample means. N.A. denotes unavailable estimates.
a. Significant at the 5 percent level.
b. Significant at the 10 percent level.
SOURCES: Panels A, B, and D are from Neumark and Wascher (1992). Panel C is from Neumark and Wascher (1994a).

mum-wage effects should be stronger for the less-skilled teenagers than for the (on average) more-skilled young adults. This prediction, however, is supported only when the enrollment rate is included. At the time, we interpreted this evidence as suggesting that the model excluding the enrollment rate was probably misspecified, as it seemed difficult to argue that minimum wages have the predicted effect for the young-adult group as a whole, but not for teenagers. We therefore concluded from these results that minimum wages reduce employment, with elasticity estimates in the range -0.1 to -0.2. In some of our later research, however, we explained how the results for specifications excluding the enrollment rate—indicating net disemployment effects for young adults but not for teenagers—could be reconciled with the competitive model in which some low-wage workers lose their jobs when minimum wages increase. We will return to this issue below.

The failure to find evidence of a negative minimum-wage effect for teenagers in specifications excluding the enrollment rate is consistent with both of Card's studies in the ILRR symposium (Card 1992a, 1992b). Thus, we do not think there is much controversy in the recent research over whether the "reduced-form" employment effects for teenagers (that is, those that do not control for shifts in enrollment) are small or near zero, when such employment effects are estimated from Current Population Survey (CPS) data. More controversial, however, is the question of whether to put more stock in the estimates controlling for enrollment rates.

In their comment on our paper, Card et al. (1994) criticized our inclusion of the enrollment rate—which is a supply variable—in the employment equation, which they argued should be interpreted as a labor demand function. But, as Charles Brown, Curtis Gilroy, and Andrew Kohen pointed out in their 1982 paper, if there is an uncovered sector or if some workers earn above the minimum wage, then aggregate employment is determined by both supply and demand. Card et al. also argued that the enrollment measure we used, which counted only individuals who were in school and not employed, generated a spurious negative correlation between employment and enrollment rates that led to biased results. We believe that this criticism was overly strong.[5] But we agree that it might be better to use an enrollment rate that also includes employed individuals. Therefore, in our reply to their comment (Neumark and Wascher 1994a), we also included an enrollment measure based on a separate question included in the CPS. Estimates using this measure are reported in panel B of table 4–1. For teenagers, the estimated minimum-wage effect (-0.11) is smaller and no longer significant, while for young adults the estimated effect (-0.16) is essentially unchanged, and remains statistically significant. Thus, for teenagers the statistical strength of the conclusions is sensitive to the enrollment rate used, although the estimated elasticity is still in the range (-0.1 to -0.2) that we reported.

Of course, the potentially more important problem with the enrollment rate—as we noted in our 1992 paper—is that school enrollment is a decision that may be affected by minimum wages and employment opportunities, and so may be endogenous. This led us, in our reply to Card et al., to compute instrumental variable estimates of equation (1), using data on school expenditures, pupil-teacher ratios, and compulsory schooling laws as instruments to control for variation in enrollment unrelated to labor market conditions. These estimates, which are re-

---

5. First, Card et al. claimed that "schooling and work go hand in hand for most teenagers" (p. 488), which we subsequently showed to be false. Second, they claimed that the spurious negative correlation between employment and our enrollment measure arose because our enrollment rate is simply "one minus the employment rate plus some noise" (p. 488). We showed that this assertion also was strongly refuted by the data. See Neumark and Wascher (1994a).

ported in panel C of table 4–1, show stronger disemployment effects, although they again are not significant for
teenagers using the less restrictive enrollment definition.[6]
These results reinforced our view that minimum-wage effects are negative both for teenagers and for young adults,
and they motivated us to investigate further the question
of the determination of employment and enrollment in
response to minimum wages (this later research is discussed below).

In addition to the question of whether the enrollment rate should be included, Card et al. raised two other
issues that they claimed invalidated our finding that minimum wages reduce employment. First, they criticized our
use of a relative minimum-wage measure—that is, a measure based on the ratio of the minimum-wage level to the
average wage in the state.[7] In particular, they claimed to
show the inappropriateness of using a relative minimum-
wage measure by demonstrating that the correlation
between the relative minimum-wage measure and the average wage of teenagers is negative, while arguing that if
minimum wages increase the relative price of teen labor,
the correlation should be positive. They then reestimated
our equation using the log of the nominal minimum-wage
level in place of the relative minimum-wage variable and
found a positive minimum-wage effect, significant when
the enrollment rate was excluded.

This argument, however, ignores the influence of

---

6. These estimates are for 1978–1989. In the original paper, there
is a typographical error, with the estimated coefficient on the original
enrollment variable for teenagers reported as 0.25, rather than −0.25.
Also, we noted in our comment that when we also correct for serially
correlated and heteroskedastic errors, the estimated minimum-wage
effects are negative and significant (at the 5 or 10 percent level) for
both teenagers and young adults, using either enrollment rate.

7. We also multiplied by an estimate of the coverage rate. A similar
relative minimum-wage measure—usually referred to as the Kaitz
index—was used in virtually all the earlier research on minimum
wages.

shifts in the nominal level of wages relative to a fixed minimum. Clearly, parallel movements of nominal wages of teens and older workers—attributable to inflation, for example—will induce a negative correlation between the relative minimum-wage variable and average teen wages.[8] The more important point is that nominal wage increases, given a fixed nominal minimum wage, should act in a similar manner (with the opposite sign) to increases in the nominal minimum wage, as the minimum wage becomes binding for fewer and fewer workers and falls in real value. The relative minimum-wage measure captures this effect.[9]

Moreover, there are important theoretical reasons for using a relative minimum-wage measure rather than the nominal minimum wage. First, we want a measure of the real wage, and the average wage is a good substitute for a price index, which is unavailable at the state level. Second, the relative price of teen (or young-adult) labor to that of other labor is likely to be the price to which demand for young workers is most sensitive.[10]

The other issue they raised with respect to the specification of the minimum-wage variable was the inclusion of lagged effects, which the results in panel A of table 4–1 (and other results in our 1992 paper) suggest are important. Because Card's (1992a) paper on regional variation

---

8. The relative minimum-wage variable and the relative (to the total or adult) wage of teenagers should be positively correlated. In our reply, we showed this to be the case.

9. In contrast, the minimum-wage measure advocated by Card et al. and used in Card (1992a) is the fraction of workers between the previous year's and the current year's minimum wage. We have no question that, following a minimum-wage increase, this is a reasonable proxy for the importance of a minimum-wage increase. But over a longer period, such a measure is likely to be less relevant, as it ignores the erosion of the real value of a fixed nominal minimum wage attributable to increases in the general level of wages and prices.

10. We showed in our reply that, in three of four specifications, the data did not reject the specification in which the minimum wage relative to the average adult wage is used.

in minimum wages used only a one-year first-differenced version of equation (1), we were interested in whether the absence of significant minimum-wage effects in his results was attributable to the failure to allow more time for minimum wages to have an effect. We first noted that if we followed Card's procedure and estimated a one-year first-differenced equation rather than using the within-group estimator to control for fixed state effects, the estimated minimum-wage effect on employment was positive or zero using our data, even when the enrollment rate was included. These estimates are reported in columns (1) and (2) of panel D of table 4–1.

We then showed econometrically, however, that the positive bias from omitting a lagged minimum-wage effect in the one-year first-differenced equation was much more severe than in our within-group estimates. This result was also borne out empirically. When lagged minimum wages were included in either our estimated equation (reported in panel A of table 4–1) or in the one-year first-differenced equation (columns [3] and [4] of panel D), the results consistently indicated negative employment effects, especially when the enrollment rate was included. Card et al. also took issue with our suggestion that Card (1992a) did not find negative employment effects of minimum wages because he ignored lagged effects. To reexamine this question, Card et al. reported estimates of a two-year, as opposed to a one-year, first-differenced version of equation (1), and they showed that these estimates, also, indicated slight positive effects of minimum wages. In our reply, however, we pointed out that estimating a two-year differenced equation is not the same as including a one-year lag of the minimum wage, since the two-year differenced equation still has an omitted lagged effect, which in our data is negative. Thus, the evidence they offered does not really address the bias caused by omitting lagged minimum wages.

Because there is no a priori reason to rule out minimum-wage effects taking a year or more to affect employment, we see no reason to be guided by anything other than the evidence on this question, which indicates that we should include lagged minimum wages in the employment equation.[11] The failure of other minimum-wage studies—using different experiments or different data sets— to allow a sufficiently long time for inputs to adjust may therefore influence the conclusions these studies reach.[12]

Minimum-Wage Effects on Employment and Enrollment

Our 1992 paper was intended to "check" whether the time-series elasticity estimates of -0.1 to -0.2 held up in state-level panel data. Based on the results in that paper and those that came out of the subsequent exchange with Card et al., we reached the following conclusions. For young adults aged sixteen–twenty-four, the estimated elasticities are in this range regardless of whether an enrollment rate is included. For teenagers, however, the results are less robust. When enrollment is included, the estimated minimum-wage effects are negative, although sometimes insignificant.[13] But when enrollment is excluded, the elasticity estimates are close to zero.

---

11. Recent work by Baker et al. (1994) conducts a careful study of this question using Canadian data and confirms that minimum-wage effects are felt most strongly about a year after minimum wages increase.

12. For example, Hamermesh (1995) criticizes Card and Krueger's (1994) fast-food study for not allowing for the longer-run effects of minimum wages that would be predicted by a model of factor demands with adjustment costs.

13. Evans and Turner (1995) claim that these negative results are attributable to using the major activity in the survey week to define enrollment, rather than an independent enrollment question (available in October CPSs beginning in 1978). However, their results stem from mixing employment and enrollment measures from October CPSs with relative minimum-wage variables from May CPSs. When data

TABLE 4-2
Estimates of Minimum-Wage Effects on Employment and Enrollment Activities of Teenagers

Panel A: State-Level Data

	In School/ Not Employed	In School/ Employed	Not in School/ Employed	Not in School/ Not Employed
Elasticities	−0.02	−0.47[a]	0.14	0.64[a]
Mean proportion in category	0.45	0.21	0.23	0.12
Effect of 21% increase in minimum on proportion in category	−0.006	−0.02[a]	0.01	0.02[a]

Panel B: Individual-Level Data

	In School/ Not Employed	In School/ Employed	Not in School/ Employed	Not in School/ Not Employed
Effect of 21% increase in minimum on proportion in category	−0.01	−0.03[a]	0.02	0.02[a]

Panel C: Individual-Level Data

	In School/Employed to Not in School/Employed	Not in School/Employed to Not in School/Not Employed
Effect of 21% increase in minimum on proportion making transition		
All teenagers	0.03[b]	0.02[a]
Non-blacks, non-Hispanics	0.03[b]	0.01
Blacks and Hispanics	0.02	0.04[a]
Initial wage at or above new minimum	0.04	0.01
Initial wage below new minimum	-0.01	0.04[b]

NOTE: Elasticities are evaluated at sample means.
a. Effect or elasticity is based on estimates significant at the 5 percent level.
b. Significant at the 10 percent level.
SOURCE: Panel A is from Neumark and Wascher (1995a). Panels B and C are from Neumark and Wascher (1995b and forthcoming) and authors' calculations.

The fact that the estimated minimum-wage coefficient for teenagers becomes more negative when the enrollment rate is included implies that the enrollment rate (which is negatively correlated with the employment rate) is negatively associated with the minimum-wage variable, suggesting that minimum-wage increases reduce school enrollment. Moreover, in our reply to Card et al. we reported that the sum of the employment and enrollment rates was negatively related to the minimum wage, suggesting that "idleness" (being neither employed nor enrolled) increased in response to minimum-wage increases. These findings suggested that minimum-wage increases induce shifts in enrollment and labor force status of teenagers, shifts that are obscured by an exclusive focus on the net employment effects of minimum wages.

Our first paper on this topic (Neumark and Wascher 1995a) documented more explicitly the consequences of minimum wages for employment, enrollment, and idleness, focusing on reduced-form effects of minimum wages on each of these. We continued to use state-level data, but we computed conditional logit estimates of the effects of minimum wages on the proportions of teenagers in each of four possible enrollment and employment activities. Panel A of table 4–2 reports the results of this analysis.[14] The first row reports the elasticities and, for ease of interpretation, the third row translates this into the minimum-wage effects on the proportion in each category, using the 21 percent minimum-wage increase recently enacted into law.

---

are used on a consistent basis (that is, for the same month), the results are the same whether the major activity or independent enrollment question is used (Neumark and Wascher 1996).

14. These estimates differ slightly from those in table 3 of our earlier article, because we have corrected a minor error in the programs used in that article. The results, however, are qualitatively very similar. We are grateful to William Evans and Mark Turner for pointing out this error.

There are two statistically significant effects of minimum-wage increases: first, the proportion in school and employed declines, with an elasticity of -0.47 with respect to the minimum wage; second, the proportion idle (not in school and not employed) increases, with an elasticity of 0.64. These two elasticities are much larger than the elasticity of net employment (the proportion in school and employed plus the proportion not in school and employed) with respect to the minimum wage, which is -0.15. The larger shifts in the proportion in school and employed and in the proportion idle indicate that minimum-wage increases induce employment and enrollment shifts among teenagers that are larger than is suggested by the net employment effects.

We argued that the results were consistent with a competitive model of the labor market in which teenagers are heterogeneous in skills, and in which workers at different skill levels are not perfect substitutes. In particular, we speculated that a higher minimum wage, by increasing the relative price of the least-skilled teenagers, increases the relative demand for enrolled higher-skilled teenagers, bidding up their market wages and inducing some of them to leave school for employment. These higher-skilled teenagers then displace lower-skilled teenagers employed at or near the old minimum, many of whom were not enrolled. Finally—although not necessarily predicted by theory—these displaced teenagers choose not to return to school, thereby ending up idle.[15] Depending on the ease of substituting higher- for lower-skilled teenagers, the net effect on employment of teenagers as a group might

---

15. An alternative interpretation is that minimum-wage increases reduce enrollments as teens leave school and queue for jobs at the higher minimum, without any displacement of teenagers already employed. We argued that the evidence from earlier research was less consistent with this possibility, although in later work (Neumark and Wascher 1995b and forthcoming) we report some evidence consistent with queuing.

be quite small. In this scenario, however, even when the net employment effect is small there are still important effects of minimum-wage increases on teenagers. We doubt that a minimum-wage-induced decline in enrollment of teenagers or displacement of lower-skilled teenagers already in the labor market would be viewed as desirable by most economists.

In subsequent research (Neumark and Wascher 1995b and forthcoming), we examined these hypotheses more directly by using matched CPS data to create two-year panels in which we could observe individual teenagers' enrollment and employment activities before and after minimum-wage increases. Using a multinomial logit model for enrollment-employment status that conditions on the relative minimum wage, lagged enrollment-employment status, and other control variables, including state and year effects, we estimated the effects of minimum wages on transitions among these alternative activities. The first set of results using the individual-level data, reported in panel B of table 4–2, confirm those found in the aggregate data. Minimum wages significantly reduce the probability that teenagers are in school and employed and significantly increase the probability that they are idle.

More important, the results reported in the first row of panel C confirm the substitution or displacement hypothesis. Minimum-wage increases lead some teenagers to switch from in school and employed to not in school and employed, with a 21 percent minimum-wage increase estimated to increase the probability of making this transition by 0.03. These workers also generally increase their hours of work. This explains why some teenagers already in the labor market are displaced. In particular, a 21 percent minimum-wage hike raises the probability of moving from not in school and employed to idleness by 0.02.

If minimum-wage increases cause the displacement of less-skilled teenagers from the labor market, we should find that those teenagers who leave school to work full-time are more skilled than those who are displaced from the labor market. The last four rows of panel C provide evidence consistent with this implication. We first disaggregate by race, conjecturing that minority teenagers are, on average, either lower-skilled or perceived as such by employers. Consistent with this conjecture and our hypothesis regarding minimum-wage effects, we find that only for non-black, non-Hispanic teenagers do minimum-wage increases significantly increase the probability of switching from in school and employed to not in school and employed. But only for blacks and Hispanics do we find significant displacement from the not-in-school-and-employed category to idleness. The 0.04 effect for blacks and Hispanics represents a 29 percent increase in the probability that blacks and Hispanics become idle.

Another way to disaggregate by skill is to compute separate estimates for higher-wage and lower-wage workers.[16] The last two rows of panel C report estimates disaggregated by whether an individual's lagged wage was at or above the current year's minimum wage, or below it. An individual whose lagged wage is at or above the current minimum should be more likely to have his or her wage bid up because of a higher current minimum wage, and therefore to leave school to work full-time. In contrast, an individual whose lagged wage is below the current minimum is more likely to be priced out of the labor market as a result of a higher current minimum wage and therefore should be more likely to be displaced from the not-in-school-and-employed category to idleness (or, in principle, to full-time schooling). These are the results we obtain, although the statistical evidence is weaker, perhaps owing to the much smaller sample size. Among the

16. We can do this for those working for a wage who are in the outgoing rotation group of the CPS, about one-ninth of the original matched sample.

higher-wage teenagers, a 21 percent minimum-wage increase is estimated to increase the probability of switching from in school and employed to not in school and employed, by 0.04 (although this effect is not significant). Among the lower-wage teenagers, the same minimum-wage increase significantly raises the probability of going from not in school and employed to idleness, by 0.04. The results are similar if we focus only on those initially at or above the lagged minimum wage, who are more likely to be covered by minimum-wage laws. Thus, the results are again consistent with minimum-wage increases leading to the displacement of lower-skilled workers from the labor market.[17]

Our examination of minimum-wage effects on employment and enrollment using microdata leads to a substantial refinement of our earlier results on the effects of minimum wages on employment of teenagers. The evidence from our 1992 paper, along with Card's papers in the same *ILRR* volume and our subsequent exchange with Card et al., suggested that minimum-wage increases have little net employment effect on teenagers. If workers were homogeneous and teenagers were less skilled than young adults, then it would be surprising to find little employment effect for teenagers yet a significant disemployment effect for young adults. Recognizing that workers are heterogeneous, however, this apparent puzzle can be explained. Among teenagers, the potentially more-produc-

---

17. In Neumark and Wascher (forthcoming) we show that these results are sensitive to the precise sample period used (in particular, the results are not robust when we look at smaller subperiods). The results are robust, however, to using an enrollment rate definition based on an independent enrollment question, rather than the major activity in the survey week. We also show that the enrollment-employment results using the state-level data are robust to using either of these methods to define enrollment, in contrast to claims by Evans and Turner (1995). Again, their contrary results are attributable to mixing May and October CPS data (Neumark and Wascher 1996).

tive workers are more likely to be enrolled in school. In addition, for those on the margin between school and work there appears to be a sizable supply response to wage increases for more-skilled labor stemming from minimum-wage increases. Thus, a higher minimum wage leads to an increase in the market wage for higher-skilled teenagers, drawing them out of school and into the labor force. These workers then displace lower-skilled teenagers who are priced out of the market, with little net employment effect (although still a negative one, as suggested by the point estimates).

This same perspective may also explain why, for young adults (aged sixteen–twenty-four) as a whole, disemployment effects are stronger in standard employment regressions. Among the older individuals in this age group, the potential for a supply response among more-skilled individuals is likely to be much lower. That is, with the initial employment rate considerably higher (and the initial school enrollment rate lower), there is a smaller pool of higher-skilled workers who might enter the labor market in response to higher wages. Thus, the employment effects on lower-skilled young adults show through more clearly in the aggregate.

The results also help to explain why, for teenagers, controlling for enrollment shifts in estimates of equation (1) leads to negative employment effects. When minimum wages increase, enrollments—which are negatively correlated with employment—decline. When we control for enrollment shifts, we effectively hold enrollments constant, which reduces employment. But it is only because enrollment rates shift that employment of teenagers is left largely unchanged as a result of minimum-wage increases. Thus, while the most relevant regression from the perspective of estimating an overall employment effect for teenagers may be the reduced-form regression for the employment rate, this regression masks important effects on school enrollment rates of teenagers and on employment rates of particular subgroups of teenagers.

Finally, the evidence that the disemployment effects of minimum wages fall largely on less-skilled workers implies that the conventionally reported elasticities of employment with respect to minimum wages are misleading. An elasticity of -0.1—which may be the consensus elasticity at present—is generally interpreted to mean that a 10 percent increase in the minimum wage reduces the employment rate of teenagers by 1 percent. Although this is strictly correct, in a sense it compares apples with oranges. For the most part, a minimum-wage increase raises the wages only of lower-wage workers; this same group, however, experiences most of the employment decline. The conventional elasticity, then, is effectively the ratio of the employment decline averaged across all workers to the wage increase among lower-wage, less-skilled workers. A more relevant alternative elasticity might be the ratio of the employment decline among lower-wage workers to the wage increase among lower-wage workers (that is, the minimum wage increase), or similarly, the ratio of the employment decline averaged across all workers to the wage increase averaged across all workers. Either alternative would exceed the conventional elasticity, which downplays the stronger disemployment effects for those workers whom minimum wages are intended to help.

When Do Minimum Wages Matter?

The previous section considered the implications for empirical research of going beyond the simplest textbook minimum-wage model by recognizing heterogeneity of workers. Another facet of the model that is often ignored in empirical research is whether minimum wages are binding. In the textbook competitive model of low-wage labor markets, only when the minimum wage is higher than the equilibrium competitive wage should it be negatively related to employment: a legislated minimum wage below the equilibrium competitive wage should not affect employment. Thus, studies that use samples that vary with respect to whether minimum wages are binding may obtain different findings. For example, even if low-wage labor markets are competitive, some studies may reveal no effects of minimum wages on employment because they use samples in which most of the variation in minimum wages is in the range for which minimum wages are non-binding.

To estimate minimum-wage effects that are not influenced by the extent to which minimum wages are binding, we have developed methods of estimating these effects only from observations for which minimum wages are likely to be binding (Neumark and Wascher 1994b), borrowing methods from the disequilibrium labor market literature. In particular, we implement an endogenous switching regression model with unknown sample separation, with the switch point defined as the intersection of the labor demand and supply curves. In this model, observations are either on the labor demand curve (the binding regime) or at the equilibrium level of employment (the nonbinding regime, given by the reduced-form employment equation). In addition to providing more reliable estimates of minimum-wage effects, this approach enables us to ask whether variation in the extent to which minimum wages are binding helps to explain why we sometimes fail to find disemployment effects of minimum wages. Thus, the disequilibrium approach may provide another explanation for the absence of a negative correlation between employment rates and minimum wages in some studies, and hence prove useful in assessing the evidence from various minimum-wage experiments.

In panel A of table 4–3 we report the estimated minimum-wage effect and implied elasticity from the disequilibrium model, using state-level data from 1973–1989 for

TABLE 4–3

ESTIMATES FROM DISEQUILIBRIUM MODEL OF
EMPLOYMENT EFFECTS ON YOUNG ADULTS AND TEENAGERS

A. Young Adults	Minimum-Wage Effect in Binding Regime	Elasticity
	−0.33[a]	−0.21[a]

B. Young Adults	Average Probability on Binding Regime	Average Probability— Weighted Elasticity
Full sample	0.48	−0.11
1973	0.05	−0.01
1981	0.67	−0.16
1989	0.29	−0.06
East-South-Central	0.87	−0.24
West-South-Central	0.63	−0.15
Mountain	0.35	−0.07
Pacific	0.26	−0.05

C. Young Adults	Single-Equation Regression Estimates of Minimum-Wage Effects	
Prob. (binding) >0.5	−0.56[a]	
Prob. (binding) ≤ 0.5	0.34[a]	
East-South-Central and West-South-Central states	−0.14[a]	
Pacific and Mountain states	0.46[a]	

D. Teenagers	Minimum-Wage Effect in Binding Regime	Elasticity
Estimates from disequilibrium model	−0.34[b]	−0.29[b]
	Average Probability on Binding Regime	Average Probability— Weighted Elasticity
Full sample	0.50	−0.16
California, 1988 (before increase)	0.004	−0.001
California, 1989 (after increase)	0.25	−0.07

NOTE: Elasticities are evaluated at sample means.
a. Denotes that effect or elasticity is based on estimates significant at the 5 percent level.
b. Significant at the 10 percent level.
SOURCE: Neumark and Wascher (1994b) and authors' calculations.

young adults (aged sixteen–twenty-four).[18] The estimated effect (-0.33) is negative and significant, and more than twice as large as the estimate from the corresponding "single-equation" estimate (-0.14, not reported in the table).[19] This estimate implies that when minimum wages are binding, the elasticity of employment with respect to the minimum wage is -0.21.

The model estimates can also be used to estimate the probability that observations are on the alternative regimes, with some representative estimates shown in column (1) of panel B. In addition, column (2) presents the average probability-weighted elasticity of employment with respect to minimum wages, computed as the average across observations of the standard elasticity multiplied by the probability that the minimum wage is binding for an observation. For the full sample, as the first row of panel B shows, the average probability that the minimum wage is binding is 0.48, and the average probability-weighted elasticity is -0.11.

The remaining rows of panel B provide evidence on the variation in the probability that minimum wages are binding (and variation in the elasticities) across years and regions. For example, in 1981, after the minimum wage rose to \$3.35, the estimated probability that minimum wages were binding was 0.67. But by 1989, with the federal minimum wage stagnant (although some states had raised their minimums), this probability fell to 0.29. Similarly, there is considerable variation across regions. For example, in the low-wage South Central states, the estimated probabilities that minimum wages are binding are higher than in the high-wage Mountain and Pacific states.

---

18. In this research, we revert to treating workers within the same state and year as homogeneous. It remains for future research to fully integrate worker heterogeneity with this disequilibrium approach.

19. These results are for specifications using the contemporaneous minimum-wage variable but not the lagged variable, and excluding enrollment rates.

This variation in the probability that minimum wages are binding, along with the difference between the estimated minimum-wage effect on the binding regime and the single-equation estimate of the minimum-wage effect for the whole sample, suggests that standard single-equation regression estimates of minimum-wage effects may be quite sensitive to the extent to which minimum wages are binding in a particular sample. The estimates reported in panel C document this sensitivity in our data. The first two rows divide the sample based on whether the estimated probability that the minimum wage is binding is above or below 0.5. For the subset of observations with a relatively high probability that the minimum is binding, we obtain a significant negative estimated minimum-wage effect. In contrast, for those observations with a low probability that minimum wages are binding, we obtain a significant positive effect.[20] A similar result is reflected in the next two rows of panel C, where we report single-equation estimates for the states with the highest and lowest estimated probabilities that minimum wages are binding. For the former, the estimated minimum-wage effect is significant and negative, and for the latter, the estimated minimum-wage effect is significant and positive. These estimates strongly suggest that studies may conclude erroneously that minimum wages do not reduce employment if the samples that they use are heavily weighted toward observations for which minimum wages are relatively less likely to be binding.[21]

---

20. Conversely, if we estimate the disequilibrium model for these two subsamples, we should still find negative effects of minimum wages in the binding regime in both subsamples. In Neumark and Wascher (1994b) we show that this is the case.

21. In Neumark and Wascher (1994b) we also estimate a multiple-regime model allowing for monopsony, which is one interpretation of a positive minimum-wage coefficient. Alternatively, the positive effects in panel C of table 4–3 may reflect states raising minimum wages that are largely nonbinding when youth labor markets are robust.

Panel D of the table reports the minimum-wage effect from the disequilibrium model estimated for teenagers, who have been the focus of most of the recent research on minimum wages. The estimated disemployment effect when minimum wages are binding is −.34, and it is significant at the 10 percent level. The implied elasticity is −0.29, somewhat larger than the elasticity for the broader young-adult group. As the second row of the panel shows, the average estimated probability that minimum wages are binding for teenagers is 0.50, and the average probability-weighted elasticity is −0.16.

Finally, to provide some idea as to how variation in the probability that minimum wages are binding may affect results from other studies, the last two rows report the estimated probability that minimum wages were binding for teenagers in California immediately before and after the 1988 minimum-wage increase studied by Card (1992b).[22] Before the minimum wage rose, the estimated probability that the minimum wage was binding was 0.004, with an implied elasticity of essentially zero. After the minimum wage rose, the probability rose to 0.25—one-half the average probability for the sample as a whole—with a probability-weighted elasticity of −0.07. This suggests that, even after the 1988 minimum-wage hike in California, the minimum wage did not have much "bite."

In sum, the application of disequilibrium models of the labor market to estimating minimum-wage effects helps to address an important shortcoming of the more traditional single-equation approach. In particular, the competitive model with homogeneous labor implies that minimum-wage effects will be evident only when minimum wages are binding. This, in turn, suggests that the estimated minimum-wage effects from single-equation reduced-form regressions will be sensitive to the sample

---

22. The minimum wage rose in July 1988, whereas our observations are for May of each year.

used. On the one hand this is unfortunate, as it implies that studies of minimum-wage effects based on relatively narrow samples may be uninformative as to general questions regarding the effects of minimum wages on employment. On the other hand, this is exactly what the theory predicts.

The New Jersey–Pennsylvania Minimum-Wage Study

Our research described in the preceding sections questions the basic approach of estimating minimum-wage effects from simple regressions of employment on minimum wages, and shows that approaches that are better integrated with the competitive model of low-wage labor markets lead to evidence more consistent with this model. In contrast, our most recent paper (Neumark and Wascher 1995c) raises questions about the data used, and the conclusions reached, in what is probably the most influential "revisionist" study: Card and Krueger's (1994) study of fast-food establishments in New Jersey and Pennsylvania before and after the minimum wage in New Jersey rose from \$4.25 to \$5.05. Card and Krueger's experiment is to conduct a "differences-in-differences" comparison of relative employment changes in New Jersey and Pennsylvania, to test the prediction that minimum-wage increases reduce employment of affected workers. Contrary to this prediction, they find "no evidence that the rise in New Jersey's minimum wage reduced employment at fast-food restaurants in the state," and even that "the increase in the minimum wage increased employment" (p. 792). We have uncovered serious problems with their data, however, and we have found that more reliable data lead to the opposite conclusion.

The most obvious problem is indicated by comparing the variability of employment change in Card and Krueger's data, which were obtained from telephone surveys, and in our data, which were obtained from payroll records supplied by franchisees or parent corporations.[23] In particular, there are some extremely large employment changes in Card and Krueger's data. For example, in Pennsylvania, the ninetieth centile of the employment change distribution is 11.8, while the tenth centile is − 17.5, for a ninetieth–tenth centile difference of 29.3; in New Jersey the ninetieth–tenth centile difference is 18.5. This variability of employment change seems inordinately high, given that the mean level of employment in Card and Krueger's survey was 21. In contrast, in the payroll data, the ninetieth–tenth centile differences are 7.8 in Pennsylvania and 8.1 in New Jersey.

Our sense is that the excess variability in Card and Krueger's data is attributable to the imprecise nature of their survey questions eliciting the employment levels. The interviewer reached a manager or assistant manager and then asked, "How many full-time and part-time workers are employed in your restaurant, excluding managers and assistant managers?" Survey respondents were not given any time period over which to define employment, and their answers may well have ranged from employment on the shift during which the telephone survey took place, to employment over an entire payroll period. Moreover, because different managers may have been interviewed in the two waves of the survey (before and after New Jersey's minimum-wage increase), there is no reason to believe that the responses in the first and second waves are based on the same "definition" of employment. In contrast, the payroll data are based on data submitted by restaurant owners on the total number of hours worked by nonmanagement employees on a weekly, biweekly, or monthly basis, which we converted into weekly full-time equivalent

---

23. For the samples discussed here, Card and Krueger's data set contains 385 observations, while ours contains 230 observations. In Neumark and Wascher (1995c) we provide details of the data collection procedure.

employees (FTEs) assuming a full-time workweek of thirty-five hours. Thus, the payroll data measure employment for a well-defined payroll period, on a consistent basis for the two survey periods.

The apparent differences in the quality of data from the two sources have substantive consequences for the differences-in-differences estimates of the effect of the New Jersey minimum-wage increase. Card and Krueger's data indicate that, on average, over a period of about eight months following New Jersey's minimum-wage increase, employment at fast-food restaurants in New Jersey grew by 3.39 more full-time equivalents (FTEs) than in Pennsylvania, a difference that is statistically significant and implies an elasticity of employment with respect to the minimum wage of 0.93.[24] In contrast, the payroll data indicate a statistically significant relative employment *decline* in New Jersey of 0.76 FTEs, implying an elasticity of −0.24. This latter evidence is consistent with the findings from our other research, and with the prediction of the competitive model of low-wage labor markets.

Conclusions

In the course of presenting our research on minimum wages, it was frequently suggested to us that evidence of nonnegative or even positive employment effects of minimum wages simply could not be correct, because it was inconsistent with the theory. While we certainly believe that the competitive theory of labor demand should not be discarded capriciously, we also share the perspective—with our opponents in this debate—that the ultimate test

---

24. This estimate is based on the subsample of restaurants (distinguished by chain, ownership, and location) in the universe from which the payroll data were drawn. If we use Card and Krueger's full sample and include management employees, the estimated effect is also statistically significant, although the elasticity is slightly smaller (0.70).

of the theory is the data, and we should stand ready to modify or replace a theory if it is convincingly rejected. We differ with them, however, in our assessment of whether the theory has been rejected. As the preceding review of our research makes clear, we do not think that the recent research on minimum wages has yielded convincing evidence that is inconsistent with the competitive model of labor markets and its prediction that—under some circumstances and for particular groups of workers—raising the minimum wage will reduce employment.

We think it is safe to say that the best-known study reporting evidence against the competitive model is Card and Krueger's New Jersey-Pennsylvania study of the fast-food industry, which suggests that raising the minimum wage resulted in higher employment. We have shown, however, that a more reliable data source for this experiment indicates that relative employment fell in New Jersey following that state's minimum-wage increase.

Card's studies of the California minimum-wage increase in 1988 and the federal increase in 1990, along with our study of federal and state minimum-wage increases over a longer period, fail to find evidence of negative reduced-form effects of minimum wages on employment of teenagers, although we find negative effects for the broader group of sixteen–twenty-four-year-olds. Our research has identified two potential explanations of these findings, however, both of which are consistent with the competitive model.

First, minimum wages are not always binding. When samples are comprised of observations in which minimum wages are relatively unlikely to be binding, we do not find disemployment effects, as theory would predict. For observations on states and years in which minimum wages are likely to be binding, however, we find evidence that minimum wages reduce employment of teenagers and young adults.

Second, minimum-wage increases induce substitution of higher-skilled for lower-skilled teenagers. That is, such increases reduce the employment of low-skilled teenagers, but increase the supply of higher-skilled teenagers, whose wages are bid up owing to the increased price of low-skilled labor. This supply response moderates the total disemployment effect, and there is no reason to believe that the total effect should be significantly negative.

Thus, our provisional conclusion from the new minimum-wage research—our own included—is that the revisionist evidence is not compelling, and that much of the conflicting evidence can be reconciled with the competitive view of minimum wages and low-wage labor markets. At the same time, we should emphasize that we do *not* claim to have reconciled all the existing research findings. With the possible exception of the New Jersey-Pennsylvania study, we have not conclusively demonstrated that these studies obtained the wrong answer because of problems with either methods or data. Rather, we have offered hypotheses and supporting evidence suggesting why these studies might have failed to confirm the conventional view of minimum wages, even if that view is correct. But we also think there is more to be learned about the economics of minimum wages and labor demand from replications of the types of studies on which the revisionist evidence is based, and from additional testing of our hypotheses regarding the sources of variation in estimated minimum-wage effects.

5

The Old Minimum-Wage
Literature and Its Lessons
for the New

Charles C. Brown

R esearch on the minimum wage has come in waves. The most recent wave is well described in chapters 2, 3, and 4. An earlier wave began around 1980 and was published shortly thereafter, much of it stimulated by the Minimum Wage Study Commission and a substantial project organized by the American Enterprise Institute. I will focus here on the literature on the employment effects of the minimum wage as it stood as the most recent wave of research began. In addition to the main conclusions of that literature, I will try to emphasize its puzzles and problems and the implications of the "old" literature for current work.

Time-Series Studies

Most research on employment effects of minimum wages has used time-series data. The dependent variable was the faction of teenagers who are employed in each period (typically, quarterly data are used) from the CPS. The key explanatory variable was usually the Kaitz index, the ratio of the minimum wage to the average wage multiplied by coverage. The focus on teenagers reflected the fact that, among the population groups whose employment status was reported by CPS each month, teenagers were most likely to hold minimum-wage jobs. Perhaps surprisingly, monthly or quarterly data on those with low levels of education were unavailable.

In general, employment elasticities were in the -0.1 to -0.3 range, so a 10 percent increase in the minimum wage reduced teen employment by 1 to 3 percent (table 5–1). Focusing on the more recent studies, which included the experience of the 1970s and controlled for more determinants of teen employment besides the minimum wage, leads one toward the lower end of that range—1 percent rather than 3 percent.

In the early 1980s there was a surprising degree of consensus. I was on the staff of the Minimum Wage Study Commission when Curtis Gilroy, Andrew Kohen, and I reached the conclusion described above. At the same time a parallel effort was sponsored at AEI. As Mary Eccles and Richard Freeman (1982) observed when the commission report and the AEI volume appeared, the findings from these two efforts were quite similar. The commission's recommendations were more favorable to the minimum wage than would have emerged as the consensus view of the AEI researchers.

While the research of the past two decades emphasized effects of the minimum wage on employment, early articles focused on its effects on unemployment. As the summary of estimated effects on unemployment in table 5–1 makes clear, there is a stunning decline in the estimated unemployment effects over time.

We should have been looking at the employment effects all along. If the minimum wage reduces employment but the number of teens looking for work is also reduced, this hardly makes the minimum wage an attractive policy. Conversely, if the minimum wage has small effects on employment but it induces more teens to search for the more attractive but scarce jobs, the increase in the unemployment rate would overstate its true costs. Policy makers

TABLE 5–1
ESTIMATED EFFECT OF A 10 PERCENT INCREASE IN THE MINIMUM
WAGE ON TEENAGE EMPLOYMENT AND UNEMPLOYMENT,
1970–1991

Study	Percent Change in Teenage Employment	Change in Teen Unemployment Rate, in Percentage Points
Kaitz (1970)	–.98	–.01
Adie (1971)		2.53
Moore (1971)		3.65
Kosters-Welch (1972)	–2.96	
Lovell (1972)		–.00
Adie (1973)		.52
Lovell (1973)		–.25
Kelly (1975)	–1.20	
Gramlich (1976)	–.94	
Kelly (1976)	–.66	
Hashimoto-Mincer (1970); Mincer (1976)	–2.31	.45
Welch (1976)	–1.78	
Ragan (1977)	–.65	.75
Mattila (1978)	–.84	.10
Freeman (1979)	–2.46	.00
Wachter-Kim (1979)	–2.52	.51
Iden (1980)	–2.26	
Abowd-Killingsworth (1981)	–2.13	
Betsey-Dunson (1981)	–1.39	
Hamermesh (1981)	–1.21	
Ragan (1981)	–.52	
Brown-Gilroy-Kohen (1983)	–1.14	.01
Solon (1985)	–.99	
Wellington (1991)	–.63	

SOURCE: Brown, Gilroy, and Kohen (1981), updated by author.

often still focus on unemployment effects, however, and even confuse reduced employment with increased unemployment, when discussing changes in the minimum-wage law. Gradually, the focus of official discussion has followed the academic literature in emphasizing employment effects.

Does it matter whether one measures employment by the number employed or by an hours-weighted measure like full-time equivalents? A few of the studies here did look at this issue, but on the whole they are inconclusive. It certainly seems *possible* that measuring employment in full-time equivalents might matter, but based on the articles that reported findings both ways I cannot find any systematic difference. Since the full-time equivalent employment measure is at least as relevant for policy discussion as the number of workers employed, the lack of clear results on this score is a significant gap in the literature.

Most economists would expect that if the minimum wage hurts low-wage workers' employment and black teenagers typically will be paid less than white teenagers by employers, then we should expect the effect on black teens to be more seriously negative than that for white teens.

One can find evidence for this prediction in some studies—and not find it in just as many. The literature as a whole does not corroborate the prediction. Perhaps this is because the number of black teens in the Current Population Survey each month is not as large as we would like it to be for isolating the black-white differences. But it would be a serious misreading of the available evidence to claim the literature strongly supports the conjecture that the effects are more serious on black teens than on whites. I myself would say "no verdict" based on the available data.

In addition to converting the findings of many studies into a comparable metric—the 1–3 percent estimate that is our most cited conclusion—we spent a fair amount of time trying to look at the importance of specification differences among studies. Were the estimates affected in any predictable way by other variables one held constant, or by allowing for lagged effects of a minimum-wage increase, or by numerous other factors?

By extending the sample period through the late 1970s, we obtained results that were reasonably insensitive to a fairly wide range of specification choices. A 10 percent increase in the minimum wage reduced teenage employment by about 1 percent, plus or minus a small margin regardless of what we did (Brown, Gilroy, and Kohen 1983). This helps account for the consensus.

One important choice—though one made by most of the researchers at the time—is to combine the coverage and level of the minimum wage into a single variable. The Kaitz index is basically the fraction of employment covered by the minimum wage times the ratio of the minimum wage to the average wage. Standard models predict that increasing coverage of the minimum wage and raising its level both reduce employment. But no strong argument suggests that the product of the two would magically drive the results, and so we tried to separate them.

With a logarithmic specification of the minimum-wage variables, one can relax the restriction implicit in the Kaitz index by allowing for the different effects of the logarithms of coverage and the logarithm of the ratio of the minimum to the average wage. Relaxing that restriction gives somewhat larger negative effects in the minimum wage. The elasticities run on the order of -0.2 rather than $-.01$, so a 10 percent increase reduces employment by 2 percent rather than 1 percent. But these estimates suggest that expanding coverage does not reduce teen employment. The idea that the level of the minimum wage matters but its coverage does not is hard to accept.

Another more widely noted dent in the consensus was mentioned by Alan Krueger in his presentation. As

91

researchers extended the sample period through the 1980s, even with statistical specification exactly the same, the estimated effects of the minimum wage on teen employment became smaller, as the Wellington (1991) entry in table 5–1 demonstrates.

There has been some conjecture about why that has occurred. The main hypothesis is that by the mid-1980s the minimum wage was so low (relative to average wages) that it did not matter. Kevin Murphy has suggested that this is probably not the right answer, because wages of relatively unskilled workers failed to keep pace with average wages in the 1980s. Thus, why the time-series results declined in magnitude remains a puzzle.

What we observe is a balance of gainers and losers. Those who were a bit above the minimum before, of course, are relatively more attractive hires once the wage of their slightly less skilled competitors has been raised. But my reaction to the time-series studies, just before the most recent wave of minimum-wage research, was one of puzzlement that the estimated effects on teenagers as a group were so low.

Cross-Section Estimates

The time-series estimates were the more influential part of the earlier minimum-wage literature. The cross-section studies, however, while fewer in number and smaller in impact, are the most directly relevant for the new minimum-wage research. Several of these studies examine the ways in which employment changes differed between parts of industries or areas that were required to make large wage increases to comply with a new minimum-wage law and sectors that were much less affected. They were really difference-in-difference studies, decades before that term was invented. In general, they have had less influence than the time-series studies on the "consensus" view of the minimum wage. In part, this is because the results of the various studies differ so widely; in part, because there was little attempt to check the implicit assumption that the experience of the low-impact sectors served as an appropriate indicator of what would have happened to the high-impact sectors had there been no change in the minimum wage. While the execution was simpler and ultimately less convincing than the recent work, the basic idea behind these cross-section studies is quite similar to the Texas and New Jersey-Pennsylvania studies that began the new research on the minimum wage.

For example, the minimum wage increased in 1956 and a series of studies examined its effect on low-wage manufacturing industries. They compared establishments where wages had been low (so that the predicted effect of the new law on wages would be great) with establishments in the same industry where, based on the preexisting wage distribution, the predicted effect of the minimum wage would be low. In general, it was found that employment fell in the establishments that were more seriously affected by the minimum wage. These results contrast with Lester's (1946) analysis of employment in low-wage manufacturing industries following the introduction of the Fair Labor Standards Act.

Another series of studies analyzed the effect of the extension of coverage in retail trade in the early 1960s. Here the results varied a great deal from study to study, in part because of seemingly innocuous decisions about which periods one chooses to represent experience "before" and "after" coverage was extended.

A third series of studies focused on the response to extensions of minimum-wage coverage to parts of some service industries in 1966. This work offers weak evidence that employment in service-sector establishments whose wages were more seriously affected by the minimum wage (by virtue of having lower initial wages) suffered in comparison with establishments in the same industry not as severely affected.

Just as these within-industry studies were the precursors of the Texas and New Jersey-Pennsylvania studies, other early studies looked at entire areas with different initial wages and so different anticipated minimum-wage effects. In 1956, and again in 1961 and 1963, the Labor Department looked at employment in low-wage areas, asking whether, in areas where the effect of the minimum wage on wages was larger, employment changes were more negative. Looking at these studies as a group, it is hard to reject the hypothesis that the minimum-wage changes had no effect on employment. But the confidence intervals for this effect are probably also large, so it is hard to know how much weight to give to these studies.

Lessons for Current Research

What are the implications of these literatures for the new minimum-wage research—the lessons, the pitfalls, the unsettled issues? One important point has already been mentioned in the context of the time-series studies. Teenagers, the group we study most often, include both gainers and losers, both relatively high-wage and relatively low-wage teens.

Card and Krueger report that for the 1990 minimum-wage increase, roughly a third of the teenagers were directly affected—that is, probably would have earned less than the new minimum in the absence of law. A similar statistic for earlier increases, from rather limited data, suggests that this 1990 figure is representative. A clear understanding of the effects of the minimum wage thus requires an idea of what is happening to potential gainers as well as to those whose employment might be reduced, and it cannot be seen in time series of employment of all teenagers.

Obviously, microdata give some promise for being able to disaggregate more productively. Are the modest aggregate effects we observe attributable to relatively high-paid teens' employment increasing, and offsetting serious effects on low-wage teens?

A second issue is the crudeness of the minimum-wage variable that we had all been using—it both combines coverage and the relative level of the minimum wage in a convenient but arbitrary way, and uses the ratio of the minimum wage to average wages as a proxy for how far up the wage distribution the minimum wage is a binding constraint.

One of the puzzles of the time-series literature is the lack of any discernible coverage effect in the data. This is particularly troubling if one is interested in long-run effects of the minimum wage.

Both the old and new literatures look at relatively short-run effects. We expect to see some response over periods as short as a few months or perhaps a year or two, because in minimum-wage labor markets turnover rates are fairly high. Employers can adjust to a new desired level of employment relatively quickly. There is no large, quasi-fixed employment cost. There is no worry about having to increase their unemployment insurance benefits if they lay people off. These teenagers will predictably quit. So, if an employer wants to reduce employment by 5 percent or even 10 percent in a month or two, he or she simply does not hire anybody.

But conversely, whatever capital for labor substitution or fundamental reorganization of production occurs in response to a minimum-wage increase is probably going to take place over a longer run than either old or new minimum-wage studies can capture.

In principle, the most promising way to gauge the effect of a long-run permanent policy change is to focus on coverage changes rather than on changes in the level of the minimum wage. Long-run decisions like the capital-intensity of production depend on the minimum wage that firms expect over a several-year horizon. Given the saw-toothed pattern of the minimum wage relative to other wages, it is difficult to construct a plausible time series that would correspond to the minimum wage expected by covered firms over the next several years.

A change from being exempt from the minimum wage to being covered, however, *is* a nearly permanent change, because coverage rollbacks have occurred very infrequently. So, becoming newly covered is a relatively permanent change in the terms on which an owner can run the business.

Thus, the most promising place to look for long-run effects *should* be in coverage changes, with the expectation that they would be relatively large and easy to find. The effects of the much less permanent changes in the relative level of the minimum wage would be smaller and harder to find. But the time-series data then bites the analyst with a vengeance—evidence that coverage matters is *extremely* weak.

The difficulties in looking to coverage changes to capture long-run effects should remind us that we are typically looking at short-run effects not because they are what we most want to see, but because the more important long-run effects have proved so elusive.

The new studies of the minimum wage have generally looked at recent years in which coverage has been unchanged. Thus, they are untroubled by the tricky problem of separating effects of coverage from effects of the level of the minimum wage—but also offer little prospect of better estimates of the effects of relatively permanent coverage changes.

A third issue is the lessons of the old cross-section literature for the difference-in-difference studies that are so important in the new literature. Many of the concerns that arose in the earlier literature continue to arise in before-and-after comparisons of the difference-in-difference approach.

One of the most important problems with the earlier literature was that the low-impact establishments differed from the high-impact establishments in size or location. There was little attempt in those early studies to control for these differences, and since the data have survived as published tables rather than as original microdata, there is little we can do about it after the fact. In contrast, the new literature is much more careful to deal with questions about preexisting differences in employment growth between high- and low-impact observations—although unresolved controversies about exactly this issue are important to understanding the new work.

Another common finding in the earlier literature is that the answers are depressingly sensitive to the window over which the difference is measured. In the earlier literature it mattered whether the baseline was set a few months before or six months before the minimum-wage change, or whether impacts were measured one year later or two.

As we lengthen the period around a minimum-wage change that we study, presumably we can measure more of the long-run impact of the minimum wage. That is good. But we are also observing more cumulative noise and more cumulative preexisting trends. That is bad. If we measure the effect from the month before to the month after the minimum-wage change, it is fair to say we have not seen the whole adjustment. But concerns about preexisting trends probably do not haunt us in quite the same way they would if we were comparing employment one year before and five years after a minimum-wage increase. As we widen the window to capture more of the ultimate effect, we must worry that preexisting trends and other irrelevant factors will accumulate and bias our estimate of that impact.

One important policy issue that received little attention in the old minimum-wage literature was the effect of a lower minimum wage for youth. When I studied the issue for the Minimum Wage Study Commission, no natural or devised experiment would allow me to predict the effect of a youth subminimum on teenage employment or adult employment, which everyone was worried about. Even among economists who agreed on the effects of the minimum wage in the past, there was considerable uncertainty and disagreement about whether a youth subminimum was desirable.

In the event, the youth subminimum passed in 1989 after so much controversy was never much utilized, and its expiration was almost unnoticed. Using the subminimum involved some administrative hassle. But franchises and chain stores should have provided the kinds of economies of scale in paperwork to make the provision attractive for these businesses, if not for small, fully independent concerns. Why, if the minimum wage led to a pool of unemployed but desirous-of-employment teenagers, were employers not more eager to take advantage of the subminimum they had lobbied so hard to create?

It is too early to be sure what consensus, if any, will emerge from the latest round of minimum-wage research. To my eye, its use of microdata and of a number of competing analytic strategies has the potential to improve significantly on a literature that had seemed, until recently, to have little potential for innovation.

6

Employment and the Minimum Wage—What Does the Research Show?

Marvin H. Kosters

The main issue in arguments about minimum-wage policy has been whether raising the minimum wage harms many of those it is intended to help by making it more difficult for them to get jobs. This question has been addressed by examining research evidence on the relation between minimum-wage levels and employment. By the early 1980s, a broad research consensus emerged about the negative effects of the minimum wage on employment and the approximate size of such effects. This research consensus was expressed in the Report of the Minimum Wage Study Commission and in articles summarizing research conclusions. In their book, Card and Krueger argue on the basis of the research they develop and their assessment of earlier research that employment effects are instead negligible.

Card and Krueger's book represents a challenge to the old consensus, not a statement of a new one. Their research has probably not shifted the burden of proof, but it has reopened the question of how significant the employment effects of minimum wages are. Since conclusions based on empirical research always remain to some degree provisional and subject to revision, we expect expert opinion to change if strong new evidence becomes available. Are we now in a situation where what seemed to be a settled conclusion should be modified, or even perhaps reversed? I do not think the view that the minimum wage reduces employment for vulnerable groups should be abandoned. It is worth considering, however, why what we conclude about the evidence on this issue is important.

Although its effects on jobs have become a critical issue for minimum-wage policy, specific research results that have been developed do not address the full range of concerns about jobs that should be taken into account. Aggregate U.S. employment may be affected, for example, but analysts have generally regarded an effort to sort out the effects of the minimum wage on aggregate employment as too ambitious to attempt. Instead, they have looked at employment for particular groups. They have examined what happened to job totals for vulnerable demographic groups, typically teenagers; for particular industries, such as retail trade; or for geographic areas, such as states. The groups selected for examination are frequently those in which workers likely to be affected by a minimum-wage increase are disproportionately represented.

Many of those whom a minimum-wage increase is intended to benefit are also vulnerable to increased difficulty in getting a job. But concern about unintended adverse effects of the minimum wage is not limited to whether aggregate employment for a particular group is on balance reduced or not. Public policy concerns include in addition, for example, whether those with the lowest apparent earning capability lose jobs, even if total employment for the group as a whole is unchanged, and whether other conditions of employment have been adversely affected. Evidence on employment effects for groups in which vulnerable members are disproportionately represented has been viewed as providing evidence on whether employers actually make the kinds of adjustments that the simple theory suggests. We are not, as such, concerned primarily about whether a sample of fast-food hamburger restaurants has fewer employees after an increase in the minimum wage, for example. We are instead concerned about whether such evidence suggests that employers provide fewer jobs for people with low earning capabilities. Evidence on what happened to employment for vulnerable groups has been interpreted as indicative of whether employers exercise increased selectivity in hiring, change production methods, reduce output, and so on, or whether they instead simply raise wages (and prices) with no unintended consequences for numbers employed, skills of those able to get jobs, hours of work, duties on the job, and other conditions of employment.

One issue that arises in connection with the composition of groups whose employment is analyzed is the size of minimum-wage effects. Estimated employment effects are often said to be small. In judging what is meant by small, however, the peculiar form of employment elasticities that are estimated in minimum-wage research should be noted. Conventional elasticities are expressed as proportionate quantitative responses to price changes, when prices are changed in the same proportion for all the units in the group being considered. An increase in the minimum wage, however, affects only a fraction of people in demographic groups for whom a quantitative response is being measured. Moreover, the fraction affected by a proportionate increase depends importantly on the initial level of the minimum. Even among teenagers, for example, the proportion of workers affected by the minimum-wage increases of 1990 and 1991 was apparently on the order of one-third. In judging whether an elasticity estimate of $-.1$ to $.3$ is small, it is appropriate to take this difference in form into account. For comparison with conventional elasticity measures, we should either make an adjustment on the quantity side, to reflect only the proportion in the group whose wages are directly affected, or make an adjustment on the price side, to reflect the effect

101

of an increase in the minimum wage on average wages for the group as a whole.

Much of the empirical evidence on the employment effects of the minimum wage has been based on evidence for teenagers. This group has received the most attention not because teenagers are the only group affected or because their jobs are inherently more vulnerable, but because low wages are much more prevalent among teens. If jobs are affected, the effects are much more likely to be picked up by studying teenagers' employment. Changes that affect employment are always taking place in the economy, and it is difficult to isolate the effects of periodic policy changes, like a minimum-wage increase, for groups in which only a small proportion of workers are affected by such a change. The proportion affected is larger for teenagers, however, and the evidence for teenage workers is presumably relevant for other groups who are as vulnerable as teens because of their low earning capabilities.

Too much emphasis has probably been placed on the effects of minimum wages on total employment for groups whose employment experience has been examined. It has long been recognized that the minimum wage may make it easier for some members of the work force to get a job at the same time as others face greater difficulties. Changes in employment totals reflect only the net outcome; if people with earning capabilities that compare favorably with the minimum wage are advantaged relative to people in the work force with the lowest wages, this selection effect is not taken into account by changes in a total. The issue is not only how many fewer jobs there are but also who loses out if the employment mix changes. If school enrollment declines to offset a reduction in teenage employment that would otherwise occur, as suggested by Neumark and Wascher's analysis, there are valid reasons for concern about minimum-wage effects, even if total teenage employment is unchanged.

A second reason why too much emphasis may be placed on employment effects is that other conditions of employment may be affected. When a great deal of reliance is placed on the labor market for determining the characteristics of jobs and their pay, as it is in the United States, the minimum wage can lead to changes in the content of jobs and composition of pay in addition to influencing the availability of jobs. We rely extensively on the market to produce mutually satisfactory arrangements between workers and employers. A minimum wage places a limit on the terms of these bargains or matches that we call jobs. This limit does not constrain choices for most workers, but for a worker with relatively low earning capability, the minimum wage is a constraint. It may change terms and conditions for the job, and when total pay exceeds the contribution the worker is expected to make, it may reduce employment. Even if employment is not reduced, however, workers affected may be less well off with a pay package that is skewed toward a larger wage component in order to satisfy a minimum-wage requirement.

Minimum wages affect only one component of the terms and conditions of employment. Nonwage benefits, at least those that are discretionary for employers, such as health benefits and pensions, are other important elements that can be adjusted to offset increased costs of a minimum-wage increase. Other conditions of employment that can be varied include: time for scheduled breaks, tolerance of slack time, stringency of supervision, task assignment, flexibility of hours, treatment of preparation and cleanup time, and so on. Card and Krueger look at their fast-food data for possible effects on some of these conditions, and although they do not find any significant changes, employment conditions other than wages are extremely difficult to measure adequately.

Opportunities that jobs provide for learning from work experience and on-the-job training—for acquiring or improving skills that will bring higher wages in the future—are an aspect of jobs that is particularly important for young workers. To the extent that an increase in the wage that the employer is required to pay is offset by poorer training and work experience opportunities, the effects on young workers with few skills are particularly harmful, because these workers would benefit most from such opportunities, and their income needs are often less pressing than they may be later.

Card and Krueger argue that more emphasis should be placed on the effects of raising the minimum wage on incomes if employment effects are negligible. The case for raising the minimum wage is often expressed in terms of making a commitment to ensure that anyone who works hard should be able to earn a decent living and to support a family. In practice, working hard is often understood as working year-round and full-time, and a decent living is often described as earnings sufficient to attain income above the poverty line for a family of four. This viewpoint for judging minimum-wage policy—as a standard for meeting minimal needs—does not take into account any diversity in circumstances among working people. The need to support a family of four does not apply to everyone who wants to work, for example, and many jobs are also only part-time or part-year. Treating everyone as if they had the same priorities or needs is a misleading oversimplification of much more complex and varied interests.

Reducing inequality in the distribution of income is a goal related to poverty reduction in the context of minimum-wage policy. The effects of an increase in the minimum wage on the distribution of income have been analyzed, and most analysts have concluded that raising the minimum wage is a very inefficient way to reduce household or family income inequality. Although Card and Krueger apparently do not disagree with this view, they present data suggesting that the 1990 increase in the minimum wage had effects on incomes that were disproportionately concentrated in the lower part of the distribution. As pointed out by Burkhauser, Couch, and Wittenberg (1996), however, the apparent concentration of minimum-wage effects in the bottom third of the income distribution is largely a result of looking only at working people in low-income families, where only a small proportion work, instead of at all low-income families.

The controversy about the size and significance of minimum-wage effects on employment can be expected to stimulate new research to clarify the character and importance of employment adjustments. But what can we conclude on the basis of current research evidence? Most of the research evidence that has accumulated over the years has pointed to negative and significant employment effects for the most vulnerable groups. The results of more recent studies, notably those carried out by Deere, Murphy, and Welch and by Neumark and Wascher, are consistent with this view. On the basis of their studies, Card and Krueger argue that employment effects for the groups they examine have been negligible, and perhaps even positive, with the implication that it is reasonable to disregard the possibility of other, more subtle negative employment consequences of minimum-wage increases. It is necessary to make a judgment about the validity of these conflicting claims that have been made on the basis of different research results.

In my judgment, raising the minimum wage can be expected to harm the job prospects of those whose wages would be most affected by a minimum-wage hike, those who would otherwise earn the least. The evidence in studies put forward by Card and Krueger in support of their view is not sufficiently persuasive to overturn conclusions that were reached on the basis of an accumulation of earlier research and more recent studies that have also produced evidence of negative employment effects. Effects on employment of minimum-wage increases have not been easy to find in noisy data, especially for modest increases in the legal minimum from an initial level that is relatively low, so that only a small proportion of workers in potentially vulnerable groups is affected. Although the studies carried out by Card and Krueger make use of sophisticated analytical techniques, the methodology they use and the cases they examine are subject to many of the same problems and limitations as other, earlier studies. Moreover, the arguments that have been made for modifying the standard theory so that negative employment effects are no longer predicted are not very convincing.

In my judgment, the empirical evidence that is available now, taken together, should lead us to reject the view that adjustments by employers in response to increasing the minimum wage can be disregarded because they are likely to be small and insignificant. I believe, instead, that the evidence of negative employment effects is sufficiently strong that we should be concerned about the unintended adverse effects of raising the minimum wage on the availability and characteristics of jobs for those whose wages would be most affected.

References

Abowd, John, and Mark Killingsworth. "Structural Models of Minimum Wage Effects: Analysis of Wage and Coverage Policies." In *Report of the Minimum Wage Study Commission*, vol. V. Washington, D.C.: U.S. Government Printing Office, 1981, pp. 143–70.

Adie, Douglas. "The Lag in Effect of Minimum Wages on Teenage Unemployment." In *Proceedings of the Twenty-fourth Annual Meeting, Industrial Relations Research Association, New Orleans, 1971*, pp. 38–46.

———. "Teen-Age Unemployment and Real Federal Minimum Wages." *Journal of Political Economy*, vol. 81, March/April 1973, pp. 435–41.

Baker, Michael, Dwayne Benjamin, and Shuchita Stanger. "The Effects of Minimum Wages in the Canadian Labor Market: 1975–1993." Mimeograph, University of Toronto, 1994.

Betsey, Charles L., and Bruce H. Dunson. "The Federal Minimum Wage Laws and Employment of Minority Youth." *American Economic Review*, vol. 71, May 1981, pp. 379–84.

Boschen, John, and Herschel I. Grossman. "The Federal Minimum Wage, Inflation, and Employment." NBER working paper no. 652, April 1981.

Brown, Charles, Curtis Gilroy, and Andrew Kohen. "The Effect of the Minimum Wage on Employment and Unemployment." *Journal of Economic Literature*, vol. 20, June 1982, pp. 487–528.

———. "Time-Series Evidence of the Effect of the Minimum Wage on Youth Employment and Unemployment." *Journal of Human Resources*, vol. 18, Winter 1983, pp. 3–31.

Burkhauser, Richard V., Kenneth A. Couch, and David C. Wittenberg. "Who Gets What from Minimum Wage Hikes: A Re-Estimation of Card and Krueger's Distributional Analysis in *Myth and Measurement: The New Economics of the Minimum Wage.*" *Industrial and Labor Relations Review,* vol. 49, April 1996, pp. 547–52.

Card, David. "Using Regional Variation in Wages to Measure the Effects of the Federal Minimum Wage." *Industrial and Labor Relations Review,* vol. 46, October 1992a, pp. 22–37.

———. "Do Minimum Wages Reduce Employment? A Case Study of California, 1987–1989." *Industrial and Labor Relations Review,* vol. 46, October 1992b, pp. 38–54.

Card, David, Lawrence F. Katz, and Alan B. Krueger. Comment on David Neumark and William Wascher, "Employment Effects of Minimum and Subminimum Wages: Panel Data on State Minimum Wage Laws." *Industrial and Labor Relations Review,* vol. 47, April 1994, pp. 487–96.

Card, David, and Alan B. Krueger. "Minimum Wages and Employment: A Case Study of the Fast-Food Industry in New Jersey and Pennsylvania." *American Economic Review,* vol. 84, 1994, pp. 772–93.

———. *Myth and Measurement: The New Economics of the Minimum Wage.* Princeton, N.J.: Princeton University Press, 1995.

———. "Time-Series Minimum Wage Studies: A Meta-analysis." *American Economic Review,* vol. 85, May 1995.

Castillo-Freeman, Alida J., and Richard B. Freeman. "When the Minimum Wage Really Bites: The Effect of the U.S.-Level Minimum on Puerto Rico." In George Borjas and Richard Freeman, eds., *Immigration and the Work Force.* Chicago: University of Chicago Press, 1992.

Currie, Janet, and Bruce Fallick. "A Note on the New Minimum Wage Research." NBER working paper no. 4348, 1993.

Deere, Donald, Kevin M. Murphy, and Finis Welch. "Employment and the 1990–1991 Minimum-Wage Hike." *American Economic Review Papers and Proceedings,* vol. 85, May 1995, pp. 232–37.

Eccles, Mary, and Richard Freeman. "What! Another Minimum Wage Study?" *American Economic Review,* vol. 72, May 1982, pp. 226–32.

Ehrenberg, Ronald G. "Review Symposium: *Myth and Measurement: The New Economics of the Minimum Wage.*" Comments by Charles Brown, Richard B. Freeman, Daniel S. Hamermesh, Paul Osterman, and Finis R. Welch. *Industrial and Labor Relations Review,* vol. 48, July 1995, pp. 827–49.

Evans, William N., and Mark Turner. "Minimum Wage Effects on Employment and School Enrollment: Comment." Mimeograph, University of Maryland, 1995.

Freeman, Richard. "Economic Determinants of Geographic and Individual Variation in the Labor Market Position of Young Persons." In R. Freeman and D. Wise, eds., *The Youth Labor Market Problem: Its Nature, Causes and Consequences.* Chicago: NBER and University of Chicago Press, 1982, pp. 115–48.

Gramlich, Edward. "Impact of Minimum Wages on Other Wages, Employment, and Family Incomes." *Brookings Papers on Economic Activity,* vol. 7, 1976, pp. 409–51.

Hamermesh, Daniel S. "Minimum Wages and the Demand for Labor." NBER working paper no. 656, April 1981.

———. "Myth and Measurement: The New Economics of the Minimum Wage": Comment. *Industrial and Labor Relations Review,* vol. 48, 1995, pp. 835–38.

Hashimoto, Masanori, and Jacob Mincer. "Employment and Unemployment Effects of Minimum Wages." NBER working paper, April 1970.

Kaitz, Hyman. "Experience of the Past: The National Minimum." In *Youth Unemployment and Minimum Wages,* Bulletin 1657. Washington, D.C.: U.S. Department of Labor, Bureau of Labor Statistics, 1970.

Kelly, Terence. "Youth Employment Opportunities and

the Minimum Wage: An Econometric Model of Occupational Choice." Working paper no. 3608-01. Urban Institute, 1975.

———. "Two Policy Questions Regarding the Minimum Wage." Working paper no. 3608-05. Urban Institute, 1976.

Kennan, John. "The Elusive Effects of Minimum Wages." *Journal of Economic Literature,* vol. 33, December 1995, pp. 1950–65.

Kim, Taeil, and Lowell J. Taylor. "The Employment Effect in Retail Trade of California's 1988 Minimum Wage Increase." *Journal of Business and Economic Statistics,* vol. 13, April 1995, pp. 175–82.

Kosters, Marvin, and Finis Welch. "The Effects of the Minimum Wage by Race, Sex, and Age." In Anthony Pascal, ed., *Racial Discrimination in Economic Life.* Lexington, Mass.: D.C. Heath, 1972, pp. 103–18.

Lang, Kevin, and Shulamit Kahn. "The Effect of Minimum Wage Laws on the Distribution of Employment: Theory and Evidence." Mimeograph, Boston University, 1995.

Lester, Richard A. "Shortcomings of Marginal Analysis for Wage-Employment Problems." *American Economic Review,* vol. 36, March 1946, pp. 63–82.

———. "Marginalism, Minimum Wages, and Labor Markets." *American Economic Review,* vol. 37, 1947, pp. 135–48.

Lovell, Michael. "The Minimum Wage, Teenage Unemployment, and the Business Cycle." *Western Economic Journal,* vol. 10, December 1972, pp. 414–27.

———. "The Minimum Wage Reconsidered." *Western Economic Journal,* vol. 11, December 1973, pp. 529–37.

Machlup, Fritz. "Marginal Analysis and Empirical Research." *American Economic Review,* vol. 36, 1946, pp. 519–54.

———. "Rejoinder to an Antimarginalist." *American Economic Review,* vol. 37, 1947, pp. 148–54.

Manning, Alan. "Labor Markets with Company Wage Policies." Mimeograph, London School of Economics, 1993.

Mattila, J. Peter. "Youth Labor Markets, Enrollments, and Minimum Wages." In *Proceedings of the Thirty-First Annual Meeting, Industrial Relations Research Association, Chicago, 1978*, pp. 134–40.

Mincer, Jacob. "Unemployment Effects of Minimum Wages." *Journal of Political Economy*, vol. 84, August 1976, pp. S87–104.

Moore, Thomas. "The Effect of Minimum Wages on Teenage Unemployment Rates." *Journal of Political Economy*, vol. 79, July/August 1971, pp. 897–903.

Neumark, David, and William Wascher. "Employment Effects of Minimum and Subminimum Wages: Panel Data on State Minimum Wage Laws." *Industrial and Labor Relations Review*, vol. 46, September 1992, pp. 55–81.

———. "Employment Effects of Minimum and Subminimum Wages: Reply to Card, Katz, and Krueger." *Industrial and Labor Relations Review*, vol. 47, April 1994a, pp. 497–512.

———. "Minimum Wage Effects and Low-Wage Labor Markets: A Disequilibrium Approach." NBER working paper no. 4617, 1994b.

———. "Minimum Wage Effects on Employment and School Enrollment." *Journal of Business and Economic Statistics*, vol. 13, April 1995a, pp. 199–206.

———. "Minimum Wage Effects on School and Work Transitions of Teenagers." *American Economic Review Papers and Proceedings*, vol. 85, May 1995b, pp. 244–49.

———. "The Effect of New Jersey's Minimum Wage Increase on Fast-Food Employment: A Reevaluation Using Payroll Records." NBER working paper no. 5224, 1995c.

———. "The Effects of Minimum Wages on Teenage Employment and Enrollment: Evidence from Matched CPS Surveys." Forthcoming in *Research in Labor Economics*.

———. "Minimum Wage Effects on Employment and

School Enrollment: Reply to Evans and Turner." Mimeograph Federal Reserve Board, 1996.

Ragan, James F. "Minimum Wages and the Youth Labor Market." *Review of Economics and Statistics,* vol. 59, pp. 129–36.

Rebitzer, James B., and Lowell J. Taylor. "The Consequences of Minimum Wage Laws: Some New Theoretical Ideas." NBER working paper no. 3877, 1991.

Report of the Minimum Wage Study Commission. Volume I, May 24, 1981.

Solon, Gary. "The Minimum Wage and Teenage Employment: A Reanalysis with Attention to Serial Correlation and Seasonality." *Journal of Human Resources,* vol. 20, Spring 1990, pp. 292–97.

Spriggs, William E. "Changes in the Federal Minimum Wage: A Test of Wage Norms." Mimeograph, Economic Policy Institute, 1992.

Stigler, George J. "The Economics of Minimum Wage Legislation." *American Economic Review,* vol. 36, 1946, pp. 358–65.

———. "Professor Lester and the Marginalists." *American Economic Review,* vol. 37, 1947, pp. 154–57.

Wachter, Michael, and Choongsoo Kim. "Time Series Changes in Youth Joblessness." In R. Freeman and D. Wise, eds., *The Youth Labor Market Problem: Its Nature, Causes and Consequences.* Chicago: NBER and University of Chicago Press, 1982, pp. 155–85.

Welch, Finis. "Minimum Wage Legislation in the United States." In O. Ashenfelter and J. Blum, eds., *Evaluating the Labor Market Effects of Social Programs.* Princeton, N.J.: Princeton University Press, 1976.

Wellington, Alison. "Effects of the Minimum Wage on the Employment Status of Youths." *Journal of Human Resources,* vol. 26, Winter 1991, pp. 27–46.

Williams, Nicolas. "Regional Effects of the Minimum Wage on Teenage Employment." *Applied Economics,* 25, 1993, pp. 1,517–28.

Index

issue of lower minimum wage
for youth, 97–98
related to unintended adverse
effects, 100–101

Restaurants, fast-food
critique of New Jersey-Pennsylvania study (Neumark-
Wascher), 82–86
differences in low-wage worker
supply, 29
employment in New Jersey and
Pennsylvania (Card-Krueger
study), 11–19, 39–40
employment in Texas (Card-
Krueger study), 18–19
wages of workers in, 4–6
See also Employment, fast food
restaurants

School leavers, 67–76
Skill levels, teenagers
employment related to minimum-wage increase (Neum-
ark-Wascher), 67–76, 85–86
heterogeneity of, 71

Teenage employment
Card-Krueger analysis, 4–6
Card-Krueger cross-state comparison, 42–43
changes with minimum-wage
increase, New Jersey and
Pennsylvania, 56–57, 82–86
changes with minimum-wage
increase (Deere-Murphy-
Welch), 33, 46–52
costs with increased minimum
wage, 7–8, 28–32, 34
cost to employ with minimum-
wage increase (Welch), 6–7
demand related to skill levels,
9, 67–76
differences in high- and low-
wage states (Card-Krueger),
42–43
effect of minimum-wage in-

creases on enrollment and,
67–76
employment and enrollment
elasticities, 67–76
factors in shift of employer demand from (Neumark-
Wascher), 8–9
focus of minimum-wage re-
search on, 7
growth in post-1992 minimum-
wage increase, 56–57
levels in New Jersey and Pennsylvania (1988–92), 7, 39
with minimum-wage increases
(Brown-Gilroy-Kohen), 91
New Jersey and Pennsylvania
(1985–92), 42
predicted effect of increased
minimum wage, 52–53
relative to youths twenty to
twenty-four (1979–93),
48–52
skilled workers, 67–76, 85–86
substitution in response to minimum wage (Deere-Murphy-
Welch), 49–52
trends in New Jersey, Pennsylvania, and Puerto Rico (Deere-
Murphy-Welch), 40–42
Teenagers
analysis of work and school
choices (Neumark-Wascher
study), 8–9
earnings above minimum, 34
income with increased minimum (1990–91), 34–35
job losses with minimum-wage
increase (1990–91), 34–35
labor costs with increased minimum wage (Deere-Murphy-
Welch), 32–34
ratio of total labor force earning minimum wage, 36–37
wage effects on employment
and enrollment, 67–76
See also Enrollment rate, school;
Workers, low-wage; Workers,
skilled teenage

117

A NOTE ON THE BOOK

This book was edited by Cheryl Weissman
of the staff of the AEI Press.
The text was set in New Baskerville.
Coghill Composition Company of
Richmond, Virginia, set the type,
and Edwards Brothers, Incorporated,
of Lillington, North Carolina,
printed and bound the book,
using permanent acid-free paper.

The AEI Press is the publisher for the American Enterprise Institute for Public Policy Research, 1150 Seventeenth Street, N.W., Washington, D.C. 20036; *Christopher DeMuth,* publisher; *Dana Lane,* director; *Ann Petty,* editor; *Leigh Tripoli,* editor; *Cheryl Weissman,* editor; *Jennifer Lesiak,* editorial assistant (rights and permission).